# Your Driving Eye

# Your Driving Eye

## R. E. FORD

THE **BOBBS-MERRILL** COMPANY, INC.
A SUBSIDIARY OF HOWARD W. SAMS & CO., INC.
*Publishers* • INDIANAPOLIS • NEW YORK

Dedicated to
M.F.
Virginia and Edward Forler
Catherine and John McGinley
who are nationally known as experts in the
field of driver training.

# CONTENTS

# Your Driving Eye

# INTRODUCTION

There is no area of everyday human endeavor in which "the other fellow" is so invariably accused of being "in the wrong" as in the field of driving. Try to imagine yourself a witness to the kind of minor accident we have all seen at one time or another where one operator is obviously to blame. Now imagine further that this driver steps from his car and calmly addresses the offended operator to this effect: "I was entirely mistaken to move through your right-of-way as I did, and I am only too willing to make restitution."

A witness to such a scene would have a right to faint dead away from surprise. But there is little possibility you will ever be called upon to witness it. For any and all mishaps on the nation's highways have a way of heating tempers to the point at which the admission of personal driving error on any side seems virtually impossible.

What is it about our driving that makes us chronically incapable of admitting error, or even of weighing the realistic possibility that we might make a driving mistake?

It would take a trained psychologist to do justice to this question; offhand, however, a few reasons come to mind. For one thing, driving a car is a highly personal undertaking. It demands considerable skill in the use of a wide range of physical and mental responses.

One's prowess behind the wheel, therefore, may be right-

11

fully construed as a fairly sound indicator of how he functions in other comparable, crucial areas of life.

A person's entire identity is somehow involved in the way he drives a car. This is, of course, blatantly apparent in the manner in which a car "cowboy" uses an automobile for showing off his dexterity and masculine strength. It is equally, if less disconcertingly, obvious in the excessive caution of drivers who would let all the world know that they and they alone have properly assessed the dangers of the road. People are naturally touchy about their performance in all key areas, whether vocational or recreational; and driving, in a sense, combines aspects of both sport and business.

But above and beyond this, the experience of driving takes place within an aura of awareness that cannot exclude a suggestion of danger. It is perhaps this sense that leads almost all drivers to give insufficient weight to the possibility of personal driving error. Since human lives are literally at stake, any overt or tacit admission of a driving fault is fraught with the implications of an admitted criminal offense.

Yet, if we are honest, all of us will confess that from time to time we have wondered—though probably not out loud—whether we are truly qualified, either by ability or experience, to cope responsibly with the many hazards of driving. It is this private sense of doubt and inadequacy that prompts us to resist the admission of driving errors, even more perhaps than the realistic legal and financial penalties resulting from accidents.

Tens of thousands of persons are killed on the highways annually; the major cause is human error. But, as we have shown, the motoring public plays down the role of personal error in its collective mind. As a consequence, there has been no concerted attack on the cause of highway fatalities and injuries. If the public were confronted with a similar situation in medicine, for instance, cries of public protest would demand a solution.

Yet the number of highway injuries and fatalities continues to increase. There is a subtle difficulty involved. Individuals among the motoring public do not consider themselves individuals. They see themselves as mere statistical entities. As such, they attach the omnipotence of fate to what may happen to them on the highway. They are not sufficiently impressed with the role of individual human error in destruction on the highway. It is in this key psychological area that the nation's network of safety councils has failed in trying to eliminate accidents due to human error.

They have dutifully taken the first step of shocking the motoring public to a state of caution on the highways. But they have not addressed themselves to the process—and it is a highly complicated one—of indoctrinating the motoring public with full knowledge concerning proper driving attitudes. Without revolutionizing the attitude of the majority of drivers on the road today, these agencies cannot hope to cure the "disease" of accidents that has claimed more lives than most known diseases since the advent of the automobile upon the American scene.

This book is intended as an approach to a "cure" for the fatal hazards of driving. Familiar faults, such as drunkenness and fatigue, have been rightfully emphasized in the continual warnings of the safety agencies. But there has been no realistic attack upon the collective thinking habits of the motoring public. It is basically a negative attitude that makes the vast majority of drivers cling stubbornly to the hazardous • driving procedures that place the lives of all of us in daily jeopardy.

So it is this collective negative psychology that must be broken down first. The most effective way of doing this is to drive home the intellectual, or rational, nature of the driving experience and not merely the mechanical considerations set forth in most discussions of safe driving. This will get the beginning driver off to a good start, and even, let's hope, soften the shell of self-righteousness that immunizes the majority of even experienced drivers to full enlightenment.

Only through a rational, or intellectual, approach to the driving experience can a driver's mind be opened up sufficiently to lead to inquiry and the assimilation of new data that will improve his driving. Of course, the beginning driver is more open to new information from the start.

This book will, therefore, lead us on a circuitous course, one that explores the rigid attitudes of veteran drivers and at the same time instills in the novice the rightful intellectual awe of the driving experience. We shall touch on the psychological factors that lie behind the obsessive insistence by most drivers who believe they know all there is to know and, consequently, are never "in the wrong."

We shall sketch out the meaning and practical value of defensive driving and the way it would promote highway safety in general and protect the reader in particular, if it were generally practiced. The concept of defensive driving encompasses all knowledge that can be put to use to help the driver protect himself and others on the road.

Therefore, we will, in passing, assess the natural laws that affect the behavior of an automobile, such as gravity, and the way this force should be taken into account by the person behind the wheel. The general framework of defensive driving will also take in the all-important interplay between various reflexes, with emphasis upon the governing role of the intellect, or what might be called judgment.

And before actual instruction in the use of the controls, their mechanical peculiarities will be suggested, again with an eye to the safest possible use of the controls. There will be particular emphasis on the role of vision in driving and on ways the driver can avoid the "natural" but dangerous use of his vision. All of this will be presented in the order that it should be acquired, prior to instructions for basic driving maneuvers.

In short, we will discuss every aspect of driving but within the framework of the defensive driving concept, which is so crucial to our safety but usually not thoroughly formulated in books of this kind. I hope that this will point to the real cause of the fatal "disease" of highway accidents—the common errors committed by all of us every day on the nation's highways.

# CHAPTER 1

# An Approach to Defensive Driving

## THE WRONG FRAME OF MIND AS A CAUSE OF ACCIDENTS

When we set out on a car trip these days, most of us feel well-protected and secure from danger. We all have an abstract notion of the familiar hazards of the road and the number of fatalities that occur over holidays. We may have recently witnessed an accident, or we even may have a close friend or relative who was recently seriously injured, possibly even killed, on the highway.

But for some reason, despite this first and secondhand information, which is always somewhere in the back of the collective mind of the motoring public, we still feel safe and serene as our sleek and almost noiseless vehicle streams along the smooth and open highway toward a happy destination.

*But is this sense of security justified? The answer is plainly, simply—and disturbingly—*NO!

It is true that one's safety on the highways depends upon a number of *known* factors and conditions, the density of the traffic, weather conditions, and so on.

*But there is one factor that most of us overlook in such safety considerations: the condition of the driver's mind. This*

17

*is an unknown. In most cases, we have not even considered it in quickly surveying the odds favoring our safe journey.*

Let us hasten to add that we are not merely calling into question a driver's sobriety or general health, and not necessarily how much experience he has had behind the wheel. We refer to his frame of mind—something subtle and more difficult to grasp.

Statistics show that 87 per cent of all accidents stem from what accident investigators call "human failure." Reduced to simple psychological terms, "human failure," in nine out of ten cases, may be reduced to the wrong frame of mind.

Exact figures are not available, but there are about twenty-five million drivers on the road today who have some sort of mental or physical deficiency that makes them hazardous influences.

Add to this disquieting picture the hazards of the road, the threat of machine malfunction, and the dangerously complex patterns of high speed traffic, and you will see why approximately two hundred thousand persons are seriously injured in auto accidents every year, one-fifth of them fatally.

You may also see that every driver is confronted with a veritable jungle of threats and dangers, hazards that may assume various guises and confront him from anywhere, leaving little reaction time to avoid catastrophe. Only a driver who deals with all of these potential dangers can be considered "safe," and he can learn to cope with them only through defensive driving.

THE DEFENSIVE DRIVER

A defensive driver is one who is as vitally and persistently concerned with this jungle of unpredictable hazards of driving as he is with the more concrete safety factors, such as the conditions of the road and the good working order of his vehicle.

As we have said, most accidents are the consequence of the unforeseen and the unanticipated. So it is not enough that we have achieved a "mastery" of the workings of our car, or have become highly proficient in "normal" driving practices.

The driver who floats along oblivious to the external threats of the road—and we can see him everywhere, chatting with a passenger, trying to drive with one hand while controlling the children with another, or admiring the scenery even in the middle of a challenging turn—is risking his own life and the lives of others.

*The defensive driver is one who exercises a total concern and a full consciousness of the wrong moves that another driver might make. He has—in advance—imagined these specific threats, and has practiced, by mental "run-throughs," the defensive action he will take to counteract them.*

Obviously, this is a full-time job, one greater even and more challenging than the mastery of the essentials of operating a car. It calls for a truly "professional" approach to driving, a well-organized system of mentally cataloguing driving errors, through experience and imagination, and working out possible defensive moves.

In the course of long experience, the defensive driver will consider his own list of possible emergencies and the defensive moves he will employ against them. He will soon come to realize that the list approaches infinite proportions. The variety and number of hazards due to human failure are as complex and fluid as highway patterns during the hours of peak traffic flow on a busy Sunday.

SOME BASIC DO'S AND DON'T'S

But there are some basic "do's and don't's" that will serve as guidelines for your own list. They will serve further to provide a more concrete sense of the kind of thing that the defensive driver learns to weigh over and over again—as if in continual dialogue with himself while on the road. They will also tend to instill the open and realistic frame of mind that is necessary to effective defensive driving.

1. Learn to spot the dangerous type of driver: the cowboy, the Caspar Milquetoast, the daydreamer, the waltzer, the brake rider, and other potentially dangerous types.

2. Do not follow too closely the car in front of you.

3. Allow space so that the doors of parked cars can be opened.

4. Allow lead space for another's turning from the wrong lane.

5. "Study" the car ahead before passing.

6. Glance to your own rear and flanks before leaving a lane or curb.

7. When approaching the "blind spots" in other vehicles, watch their front tires for an indication of a move toward your passing lane.

8. When passing a parking lane, scan your path a block ahead for danger signs—feet under parked cars, a driver behind the wheel, tail-light signals, exhaust, reflections, shadows, or other indications of possible movement.

9. Remember that many drivers may have faulty vision; be ill, with or without knowing it, drunk, thoughtless, emotionally unbalanced, or in a dangerous hurry.

10. When a pedestrian or another motorist is near, be braced and ready to execute defensive action against any and all possible normal and abnormal moves.

Considerations such as these are the full-time job of the defensive driver. By following a similar train of awareness a driver can compile his own inventory, just as we will add to this list as we go along.

# CHAPTER 2

# The Keys to Defensive Driving

### A POSITIVE ATTITUDE

A driver's desire to adopt a defensive frame of mind depends upon an ability to admit fault in himself, to engage in continuing self-scrutiny, and to acquire a realistic awareness of the *external* hazards confronting him.

*It assumes a psychological attitude that is comparatively free from tension, unreasonable fears, and the gnawing panic that prevents an appraisal of either internal or external hazards.*

As creatures of nature devoted to self-preservation, we drive intuitively, or by instinct—to stretch the meaning of the word a bit. Our reflexes and reactions will lead us around or away from objects in the path of our car. It will follow the lead of our eyes around corners or the pitfalls in the road.

But our reasoning, our mind, functions as *the* crucial factor in defensive driving. And the mind must be *free and clear* to range rapidly—almost automatically—over a great number of hazards and possible countermoves.

If the mind is free, our senses will dictate a set of impulses that will lead us through normal driving maneuvers. To prove this, try turning a corner with your eyes looking properly ahead—along the prospective path of your turn into the street your car is about to enter. Notice that your eyes—and to a lesser degree your sense of feel—tell you when to start to turn the wheel and when to release the turn.

But make this same simple turn when beset with any kind of intense emotion and you will notice that there is "interference," or a "jamming" of the communication between the senses and impulses. You may turn too late, or end the turn too soon, or move through unevenly. Fear and anxiety, resentments and frustrations, and anger and impatience can garble or confuse our reactions in even the simplest operation. When the demands of our reflexes are more complex, as they invariably are on the road, inordinate emotions can prove disastrous.

Though it is difficult to make one's emotions to order, we should strive in our driving to accentuate the positive, to be doubly on our guard during periods of stress, and to work toward conditioning ourselves positively when on the road. Only this way can we safely operate today's high-speed cars and still be free to drive defensively.

THE CONQUEST OF FEARS

In addition to the strong negative emotions of anger and impatience, there are subtler anxieties that make us hesitate —or in extreme instances—freeze at the wheel. Most often these anxieties afflict beginning drivers, but they are also more evident in women than men.

Again, it would take an expert in psychology to say exactly why a woman is more inclined to hesitate where a man will size up a situation and act decisively. To dwell too long on this point would be to open the age-old question of whether men or women are better drivers. Suffice it to say, there seems to be something in the feminine nature that causes a woman to mull over an action even after the right course is apparent to her. This instinctual caution, however, can operate in favor of the driver who uses it once he—or more frequently she—applies it to specific problems and formulates decisive responses to them. But when it floods the mind to no purpose, as is most often the case, the driver's reflexes are of as little use in an emergency as a car that is out of gear.

In speaking about intense emotions that impair the mind and make effective defensive driving impossible, it would be wise to say a word about the normal fears and apprehensions of beginning and new drivers. Some carry this initial fear throughout their whole lives, others manage only to compensate for it in various ways. All drivers suffer from it at one time or another.

Fear causes reflective avoidance or retreating movements. Fair enough, if the emergency calls for these courses of action; however, disaster can result if they are unnecessary. Fear restrains the impulses, as we have noted. It distorts our perception, triggering off wrong messages to the impulses. Only occasionally, with inept or new drivers, or with those who tend to recklessness, can fear be preventive. But to acquire a proper defensive driving attitude, all of these excessive fears should be conditioned out of existence.

THE THREE MAIN FEARS

The three main fears are (1) the fear of the car; (2) the fear of traffic; and (3) the fear of self.

Fear of the car usually disappears after the beginner has spent sufficient time behind the wheel.

Strangely enough, fear of traffic is the most common of the three, but it is also the easiest to banish if the driver is trained in traffic from the beginning.

Fear of self is usually the last to go. This naturally leaves us only if we gain more and more mastery over all the problems related to driving. The greatest advantage of a defensive driving approach is that it constantly increases our knowledge of the conditions of driving and our skills to meet these conditions. Defensive driving is, therefore, the best antidote to fear.

HYPNOTIC EFFECT

Many accidents are caused by hypnotic effect. If you have ever taught anyone to drive, you may have been confronted with this. The novice will be called upon to glance at something. Instead of glancing, he stares fixedly, becoming, in a sense, hypnotized, and thus causing the car to aim at whatever his eyes are focused upon. When this happens, the operator may become frozen at both the wheel and the gas pedal. Often the hypnotized driver may swerve irrationally. This kind of panic most often grips the novice, but even veteran drivers under certain tensions may fall prey to it.

A variation of the hypnotic effect occurs most often at night. Due to drowsiness, boredom, or distraction, an operator may be lulled into a dangerous trance by the rhythm of the car or the vision of the white center line rolling by in the darkness. There is the classic story of the driver who ran off the road and explained to the police: "I was watching the white line and the next thing I knew I was following the back of a skunk into the woods."

A driver subjected to any kind of intense fear will show clear-cut symptoms that you may have noticed in yourself or others. A fearful person will look close; grip the wheel desperately; hang onto it after a turn, hesitate to apply gas or to release it; use the accelerator erratically; brake too hard, too soon, or too fast; reach for the gear shift instead of the directional signal.

Such a driver substitutes irrational worry for realistic, specific action. Through defensive driving, the mind becomes trained to deal with *real problems*. As these are mastered, confidence grows and spasmodic, meaningless, and ineffective behavior behind the wheel diminishes.

ARE YOU POSITIVE?

Once we conquer all the various emotions that blur our reactions and our judgments, a positive driving attitude will result. Then the way will be paved for a defensive driving approach.

Psychology has taught us that we reveal ourselves, our true natures, in all intimate forms of personal expression. There are few forms of human activity as revealing as the way one drives. Observe your own behavior on the road as objectively as you have observed that of others.

Do you have a positive attitude toward driving?

1) Do you use accidents or near-accidents as occasions for cursing "the other fellow," or do you put these to good use in your defensive driving mill? Do you learn from them?

A near-miss or an accident will prompt the defensive driver to put the experience to work. He will gain further information about the kind of hazards confronting him. He will rehearse in his mind what he did to defend himself, or he will reason out a better defense that might have been even more effective under the circumstances.

2) Are you open-minded and willing to learn?

Only a few drivers are realistic or mature enough to acquire the techniques of defensive driving on their own initiative. Most of us are content to muddle through from here to there, priding ourselves on the flourish with which we can spin the wheel or how swiftly we can park.

Though it may disturb the car cowboy to think so, most "experienced" drivers know little more about defensive driving than a beginner. Beginning drivers are, in fact, even better students of defensive driving because their natural, initial fears of the road have not yet been clouded over by the misguided overconfidence that afflicts the more hardened veterans of the traffic wars.

There is not a driver alive who has not at one time or another gone the wrong way on a one-way street, run through a red light by mistake, or missed a stop sign. For every mistake like this we acknowledge, there are dozens we refuse to admit, even to ourselves. A positive driver admits his errors; he ponders what made him commit them and he tries to prevent their recurrence.

3) A positive driver knows what his human limitations are.

He knows the limits of his car's performance. He knows the limits of the law and the restrictions of the rules of the road. He is not, however, a mere dogmatist, a stickler for the rules, who is willing to risk life and limb to make a point. A positive driver is one whose first job is to drive defensively, to preserve life. He will risk being wrong, even breaking a traffic regulation, if it seems best to do so in an emergency. He will yield the right of way, even if it is rightfully his, to save his own or another's life.

4) A positive driver is responsive to his surroundings.

On freeways and expressways, he will keep pace with the flow of traffic. However, the positive driver is realistic. He will even exceed the speed limit rather than cause a traffic jam or throw other cars off the pace that is pushing them from behind.

5) A positive driver will maintain the proper frame of mind.

He will be wary of rages and inhibitions in himself. He will keep his distance when aware of them in contending car operators.

A positive driver knows that provocative moves on his part can be contagious. He avoids contests with other drivers and the impulse to use his vehicle as an expression of unhealthy exhibitions of power. He will keep his distance from those who use their cars to express an unhealthy indifference to the motoring public, or to express aggressions and hostilities.

A positive driver will have a healthy respect for the "zanies" on the road. He knows there are a number of them. He would rather survive than prove they are wrong.

A positive driver will sympathize with, or at least offer understanding of, the new driver and his problems, the inept driver, and the driver in a dangerous frame of mind.

The positive driver will remind himself that accidents are not necessarily what happens to everybody but himself.

6) A positive driver will not be content with mastering a large repertory of manual accomplishments with his auto; he will insist on increasing his knowledge of possible hazards and mentally "rehearsing" the defensive driving moves he can utilize to meet them.

7) A positive driver will know what is near his car at all times.

He will look ahead and continue to glance elsewhere. He knows that driving is, visually, a full-time job. He knows his life depends upon the effective use of his eyes in this way.

He will drive under the assumption that there is always a car beyond his vision at the "blind spots" to the sides of his path. He will always signal. He does not follow closely or hover at the "blind spots" of other cars.

8) A positive driver shows good driving form.

He demonstrates respect for lines, signals, and signs. He does not start with a lurch or stop with a jerk. He does not make unnecessary maneuvers nor impede traffic. His left turns are not cut short and his right turns are not too wide. He does not rely on his mirrors or horn when more active measures are possible.

9) He never assumes that another driver will take the responsibility for avoiding an accident. On the contrary, he is always prepared for the worst and has at his "mental finger tips" a wide set of defensive maneuvers for any and all situations.

# CHAPTER 3

# First Things First

If you are an experienced driver, think back to the time when you first slid behind the steering wheel and started up the engine. Even the most unromantic among us will admit that it was an exhilarating (not to say, accelerating) experience. But at the same time it was—and let's admit this, too—a somewhat frightening one.

From the moment we decided we *had* to learn to drive—in order to get a particular job or because we were tired of depending on others for transportation—we all had certain fleeting doubts as to whether *we* would ever be able to guide such a menacingly monstrous machine at high speeds through complex traffic patterns.

Somehow or other we put this fear in its place. Perhaps we looked around and found that others—a friend or relative whom we regarded as impossibly inept—had learned, and concluded that we could too. But more than likely, remnants of that fear remain—at least on an unconscious level—to hamper our driving technique. *This is because the three basic fears we have mentioned—fear of the machine, fear of the*

29

*traffic, and fear of self—were never effectively purged during the crucial learning stage.*

This may be the case with *you* if you were taught by a relative or friend and *not* under expert tutelage. A learning driver should be guided through the three basic fears by those who are *trained* in the psychology of beginning drivers. Only *trained* instructors could have the necessary knowledge that anyone can learn to drive, given normal mental and physical abilities.

An *untrained* instructor will be naturally anxious about what may happen when the beginner first takes control of the car. A *trained* instructor knows what to expect and what to do in an emergency. *Only the expert has the confidence that must be communicated to the beginning driver, who encounters these three basic fears for the first time.* Otherwise, they are apt to hamper his driving—in one subtle way or another—for the rest of his life.

So, the first mistake that a prospective driver can make is to choose the wrong person as a "tutor." The wife is most apt to single out her husband because she feels she needs the support of someone who will "protect" her from making a dangerous error and a person close enough to sympathize with, rather than condemn her for, any clumsiness and ineptitude.

A young man is most naturally—but not most logically—inclined to choose an older member of his family to teach him. A grown man is most apt to turn to a friend; a young girl would probably ask an older brother. Those do not cover all the choices open to a would-be driver, but they are enough to make the point.

Husbands are notoriously impatient with their wives. They are habitually quick to *overreact* to her mistakes and *underreact* to correct moves. The male insistence upon his own superiority—which serves positive functions in certain situations—can be most harmful to a beginning driver. The husband, in short, is bound to carry over the battle of the sexes to his role as an instructor.

Undoubtedly, there are countless instances of women who abandoned hope of ever learning to drive because their husbands incorrectly concluded—after a lesson or two—that they could never learn. Even wives that survive their husbands' methods of instructions more often than not become indoctrinated with a life-long sense of inferiority in driving situations, like the college student who is graduated lowest in the class.

Similar difficulties may arise between sister and older brother, or between son and father. Many unnecessary fears are confirmed or are injected into the driving experience. The whole process of the conditioning and refinement of driving responses has taken place in an atmosphere of tension and recrimination. This kind of instruction is bound to result in a *negative* attitude in the novice toward driving.

Even if the relationship between the "student" and the amateur "instructor" were ideally objective and positive, the question of the quality of the instruction would remain. Would you ask a friend, for instance, to teach you the operation of any other machine as complicated and potentially dangerous as an automobile? *Probably not, because your common sense would tell you that the knowledge you would gain would be necessarily spotty and incomplete—and more importantly—in some cases, actually wrong and dangerous.*

THE ADVANTAGES OF PROFESSIONAL HELP

Without professional instruction, the new driver cannot acquire a sufficiently positive attitude that results from purging the three basic fears during his early encounters with the machine, with the traffic, and with his own tendency to make mistakes.

Furthermore, only the trained teacher is aware of new information in the field of driving relating to accidents. With this knowledge, the "pro" can guide the beginner toward an emphasis upon defensive driving which may someday save his life.

The most logical direction to turn for instruction in any field of complex human activity is toward those who have been trained over a long period in the skills you wish to acquire, those who are schooled in the use of the machine in question, and in the most effective way of communicating their knowledge to you. This fact has become more thoroughly recognized in recent decades, as many public high schools have added courses in driving to their curricula. It is also evidenced in the sharp rise throughout the country in the number of driving schools. The best drivers on the road today are those who have been trained professionally.

Without professional help, it may take many months to learn even the rudiments of driving. Driving schools or formal driving classes provide short cuts that enable a beginner to acquire competence in four to six weeks. All this, of course, depends upon the degree of fear on the part of the novice, on his dexterity in looking ahead, on how closely together the lessons are conducted, and how much he practices.

If possible, engage an instructor with a dual-control car. A good instructor, however, does not need elaborate controls. He can drive from the so-called "suicide seat" with only an extra brake. He is able to watch your eyes and predict your mistakes before you actually commit them. He will actually permit you to make mistakes under certain conditions, allowing you to experience them under controlled conditions. *Since our conditioned reflexes are involved, the process of making the error provides the best ground for learning from it.*

Many schools or instructors use cars that are not marked outwardly in any way. These are the most effective vehicles for learning, because they provide the same kind of anonymity you will find in the normal driving situation. Marked cars telegraph a message to other drivers, prompting them to make unnatural allowances for you—or even worse—to badger you for their own entertainment. In either case, you will be less likely to acquire the all-important experience of dealing with traffic *as it really is.*

### BLACKBOARD BACKGROUND

Whether you have professional instruction or not, there are certain schoolroom concepts dealing with *natural physical laws* that should be taken into account. Some affect the conduct of your automobile, and at least five should be considered carefully before you begin to handle a car.

1. *Friction:* This, of course, involves the wheel gripping the road surface. Friction varies with the weight of the car and the speed of the car. It serves to hold a vehicle to a path of forward motion. The youngster riding no hands on a bicycle has experienced the way friction can work. And the driver who has skidded out of control on an icy surface has experienced the absence of sufficient friction.

The amount of friction—and the subsequent degree of control over the car—is, as was stated, inversely related to the speed of the vehicle. The faster a car travels, the less friction it exerts upon the road, rendering it more difficult to control.

For this reason, we should always have our foot on the accelerator, since at times—on a decline, for instance—by easing pressure on the accelerator and thus increasing the friction of the wheels on the road, the gas pedal can be used to slow the car. On a decline, the use of low gear for less engine compression and, of course, the brake also increase the auto's friction. Needless to say, our foot should always be poised to use the brake for further control in the event of hazards.

So both the brake and the accelerator can be used to keep

the speed—and the maneuverability—of the car under immediate and continuing control. It seems hardly necessary to add that coasting deprives the driver of control over his vehicle and invites disaster in moments of unforeseen emergency.

An awareness of the role of friction in driving is bound to make us more responsive to the hazards that result from insufficient friction. The lack of friction can be dangerous when we are going too fast, when the tires are badly worn, or when the road is icy, oily, or sandy.

2. *Gravity:* The automobile is a ponderous machine weighing thousands of pounds. Gravity pulls it toward the earth. There are times when this pull is greater or less than normal and demands a compensation from the controls. One such instance, obviously, is on an incline, when the pull of gravity weighs more heavily upon the machine.

More dangerous are the declines, when we may become carried away with the passive sensation of the automobile driving itself, as the power of gravity exceeds that which can be provided by the gas pedal. As mentioned above, one should be careful to avoid indulging in gravity's free ride down an incline. The degree of control you surrender for this sense of free-wheeling is greater than you imagine.

Gravity exerts a greater pull on one side of the car than the other when the highways are steeply banked. Most highways are sloped to shed rain; or at least they were frequently built that way in the past, for the same reason that houses are built with peaked roofs. The modern highways—by using less malleable paving, such as concrete—are laid out flat, except when hazardous changes in direction necessitate a banking effect. On banked roads, your impulses will compensate for the imbalance of the gravitational pull between the right and left sides of the vehicle. But the fact remains that banked highways put added stress on the tires and call for added caution on the part of the driver. Banked curves, however, are much safer than crowned or sharp, flat curves because banking denies the pull of centrifugal force. A properly banked curve can almost be taken without any hands on the steering wheel if friction is held steady with the accelerator.

The important thing to remember is that hills and flat curves call for a variety of compensating controls on the part of the operator. They are, for the most part, automatic or reflexive reactions to the "feel" of the car. *But we should be aware that accidents are more likely to occur when the vehicle is placed under unnatural stresses and make allowances in our thinking and driving techniques for this fact.*

3. *Centrifugal Force:* For driving purposes, centrifugal force involves the reluctance of the car at high speeds to follow the turn you are taking. The vehicle tends to continue in a straight line. This tendency is counteracted, of course, by turning the wheels into the path of the turn and forcing the car to follow the direction of the wheels. But a battle between the car's impulse to follow the wheels and, at the same time, to fly out of the turn has been set in motion.

The mechanics of the process are not essential to sound driving procedure. But we should, again, assist our common sense with a knowledge of the laws at work. The amount of centrifugal force is in direct proportion to the mass (or weight) of the vehicle compounded by its speed. It is for this reason that we slow down at a curve, to reduce centrifugal force to manageable proportions. Theoretically—and many fatal accidents bear out this theory every day—too much speed in a sharp turn can rip the wheels off a car or wreck the steering mechanism, or, in less dramatic ways, prevent a successful turn.

It goes without saying that every turn is a challenge in itself, a minor one, perhaps, but one that should find the driver at full alert. Because this simple precept of defensive driving is so often disregarded, turns and sharp curves continue to be a major breeding ground for serious mishaps on the highways.

4. *Momentum:* In one way or another, momentum has

figured in everything we have said, or can say, about automobiles. It involves the kinetic energy of the car, its tendency to act as a force unto itself that demands on the part of the operator a continual authority over its wayward impulses. A defensive driver knows that a car offers the same kind of challenge that a horse will. Once in motion, it has a will of its own, and this must be kept under enlightened and wise control. A defensive driver will never regard his vehicle in any other way. Once a driver relaxes the control of his intelligence, an automobile becomes a monster.

Perhaps you have seen a car parked on a hill slipping its brake and plunging on its own without a driver behind the wheel. Is there any sight that can invoke such a sense of panic? Momentum is the car's blind will. A defensive driver knows how to tame it as skillfully as a cowboy tames a bronco. The only difference is that a car is never "broken" as a horse can be. Once you relinquish control of it, it reverts to its monstrous ways.

5. *Force of Impact:* The idea of momentum leads directly to the concept of force of impact—what we feel during a collision. Fortunately, most of us in our lifetime never experience it, but many of us have come closer to subjecting ourselves to it than we care to be reminded. Force of impact is determined by the speed and the weight of the vehicle as it strikes a stationary object, or the combined weights and speeds of two vehicles slamming together. Common sense tells us that the heavier the car and the higher the speed, the greater the force of impact. Common sense sometimes deserts us, however, during moments of fatigue or excessive emotions, so perhaps during times when we might forget the factors of the force, a specific knowledge of its components—weight and speed—will serve as a trigger for caution.

# CHAPTER 4

# The Mind, the Body, and the Eyes

Before actually starting up a car, we should also have at least a casual knowledge of the mental and sensory faculties called into play by the complex mental and muscular responses of the driving experience. Among these, the most important are coordination, judgment, depth perception, vision, and reaction time.

## COORDINATION

A beginning driver's potential sense of coordination depends upon several factors. We have all noticed that in the acquisition of any physical skill—during school sports, for instance—some catch on sooner than others. This is due to more native ability or greater experience in the skills required. If we are fortunate in these respects, so much the better. However, it is perhaps worth repeating that all normally constituted persons are potentially well enough coordinated to learn how to drive.

Shifting, braking, and accelerating are all interrelated through coordination. It is our coordination that allows us to move from one control to the other, or to use several of them in an easy, flowing sequence. Coordination is involved also in elaborate turns and maneuvers. A high degree of coordination is needed at high speeds on the highways. For instance, even a slight, one-eighth turn of the wheel at moderately high speeds will throw the car into a U-turn and off the road.

Coordination is also brought into play in the relationship between braking and turning. These should be separate actions. On turns, the car should be braked before starting the turn, so as to increase control over the vehicle through added friction. Braking does not combine with turning. Coordination alone can assist us in making them separate actions, yet closely related in sequence.

### JUDGMENT AND DEPTH PERCEPTION

Besides harmony between arm and leg actions, or between leg and leg movements, driving also demands the more complex interplay between our vision, our judgment, and our muscular responses. *Judgment,* even more than coordination, is acquired only after many sessions behind the wheel. The kind of judgment needed in passing cars, for instance, also involves a specific function of the eyes, called *depth perception,* or the ability to measure accurately relative distances while in motion.

Knowing the width of lanes and automobiles is helpful at the beginning in conditioning judgment. The average width of today's cars is 5½ feet. Standard makes vary in width from 4½ to 6½ feet and in length from 14½ to 20 feet. The distance between the inside of both wheel tracks on standard cars is between 4 and 5 feet.

If you glance at the wheel track of a car directly ahead, you can estimate the width of the lane you are moving through. With lanes 9 to 10 feet in width, there is a 3 to 4 foot clearance on either side for oncoming or side traffic.

It is also worth noting that by looking down over the hood, there is the distance equal to a car length between your front bumper and any point you can see on the road surface. Most drivers are surprised by the length of this "blind spot." *Since it is useless to look closely at nothing but your hood, proper instruction trains drivers to do what at first does not come naturally: to look up and away in the direction of the car's progress. Vision:* This brings us to the all-important question of vision. We are not so much concerned with how good a person's eyesight is, for with the use of corrective lenses, most of us can be qualified to pass the eye test for a driving license. *We are concerned, however, with the way the eyes are used in driving. There is no greater problem confronting a new driver than that of learning new ways of "seeing."*

This is all the more difficult because the demands for correct vision in driving often seem to contradict our impulses and training. We have already mentioned the futility and the ineffectuality of looking close and down toward the road surface. Most beginning drivers—you may have already noticed this—lean forward and carefully study whatever they can see most directly in front of them, like a person picking his footing carefully through a dark forest at night.

But in driving, your eyes are best used by looking up and forward in the direction your car is traveling. There is reflexive coordination between the vision used in this way and the hands on the steering wheel. If you look too closely, this harmony between the sense of sight and touch so essential to effective driving is impaired. We can feed our minds with the necessary visual data only by looking up and forward. Your hands on the wheel tend automatically to direct the car toward the center of your vision, as indicated earlier.

*Your vision can best be used by concentrating your sight*

*a block ahead, at a car, at tree tops, or signal lights. In this way, you will always have at your disposal a clear field of vision fanning out to either side from the point of focus directly ahead.*

The windshield is designed with its arch to allow you to do just this. For the moment, consider your eyes a camera. If a camera is held close to the ground, little information is imparted to the film. It is the same when your eyes are focused close and downward—a natural fearful tendency of the beginning as well as many experienced drivers. If your eyes offer the mind a small picture, the impulses will respond to the information in the small picture. But you are actually moving through a large picture. By looking high, you get the picture that your impulses need to work with.

Looking too closely also sets up a tension that impairs your reflexes. To illustrate this point, extend one hand with the palm toward the face. Bring the hand close to the eyes. When the hand is three or four inches away from the eyes, notice the pull on the eye muscles. If you stare long enough, you will actually feel pain. Contraction of the eye muscles causes a tension that is sent through the entire nervous system. While using your eyes in this way, you cannot possibly be relaxed enough to allow full play to all the faculties involved in driving. *Improper use of the eyes is the greatest single cause of driving fatigue.*

Watching oncoming traffic or center line is the basis of highway hypnosis and one cause of head-on collisions, and evidence of the fact that even most experienced drivers do not use their eyes correctly. They balk at the idea of keeping the eyes—under routine driving conditions—up and away from the hood of the car. This is simply because they have not been trained in the use of the fringe, or peripheral, area of their vision and therefore do not sufficiently trust it to guide them correctly. But the fact is that the car will safely follow the direction of your eyes. If you allow the proper distance between your car and the car ahead, you will naturally see in time any threat directly in your path. Your proper concern should be with an area at least a block ahead in the car's path.

More specifically, in the city a driver should look as far ahead as the traffic will permit. On a boulevard which is usually curving, he should look ahead to the next bend, and his impulses will automatically be preparing in advance to follow the path of his vision. On the highway, look ahead as far as you can see—ideally, to the horizon.

THE DRIP PATH

One way of judging if your car is properly positioned in its lane is by evaluating its relationship to "the drip path," the line formed by oil leaks in the middle of the lane. Driving lanes vary greatly in width, but your car will be centered in the lane if you straddle the drip path. If the car is in proper position, the driver should be able to see the path with the lower fringe of his vision over the 11 o'clock position of the steering wheel. Furthermore, since head-on collisions are often caused by drivers who are watching the oncoming traffic, the process of following the drip path provides beginning drivers with additional assurance.

YOUR DRIVING EYE

Almost all drivers to some extent make the mistake of focusing on oncoming traffic, the center line, some part of their own car, parked cars, pedestrians, or anything appearing close to their path. These sights should all be handled with the fringe or periphery of your vision, leaving your focus free to feed data about what is ahead in the distance to the impulses.

It is a natural tendency to be overly concerned about oncoming or rear-view traffic. But the greatest dangers lie directly in the path of the car's progress, or to the right. In a so-called free lane, your legitimate concern should be cars that might cut into your path. Where there is congestion, involving parked cars for instance, you must be alert for pedestrians, for cars stopping to park, for cars pulling out of parking lanes, and for car doors opening. So you should favor the right fringe of your vision in urban traffic, unless driving in the extreme left lane on a one-way street. In any case, utilize your fringe and keep looking ahead. Another point about congested areas, where unseen hazards are more numerous —the faster you drive, the less you see; the slower you drive, the more you see.

The most important skill a driver, new or experienced, can acquire to make him an effective defensive driver is the ability to see correctly.

*To improve your driving eye, you must improve your fringe vision and condition your mental and physical responses to react with confidence to impulses from the fringe.*

This may be difficult for the driver who has spent most of his days on the road staring at things that are no threat at all or less of a threat than might be perceived were he using his vision correctly. Many drivers — certainly all beginning drivers—have all they can do at first to cope with a car right in front of them. But a driver should work to change this, no matter how hesitant he might be to give up old ways of seeing, for the fringes of your vision can be sharpened.

IMPROVING THE FRINGE

Your fringe vision can be improved by use. You can prove this to yourself by an experiment with your television set at home. Sit across the room and center your vision upon the TV picture. Without shifting your eyes from the center, see how many objects you can pick up in the picture in a given second of time. Probably you won't pick up too many at first, but with practice you can increase your fringe vision until you can see immediately everything in the TV picture without shifting the focal point of your vision from object to object. You can increase the acuity of your fringe vision that simply. In one respect, the ideal way of instructing beginners to drive would be to equip them with blinders and at the same time with a telescopic lens to force them to focus up and out, training their fringe vision to work effectively.

The greatest stumbling block to good defensive driving technique is the poor use of fringe vision. The majority of highway accidents could have been—or could be in the future—eliminated if drivers were trained to use their eyes properly. No driver is too old or experienced to ask himself: "Have I been using the full range of my vision during my years of driving?"

REACTION TIME

Reaction time is the length of time it takes your reflexes to respond to a visual impression. Reaction time for the average person is about three-fourths of a second. If the fringe is fully trained, however, this time can be reduced to one-fourth of a second. For reasons which are highly complicated but which driving experience has confirmed, the reflexes react more swiftly to impressions caught in the fringe of vision. The reactions to fringe impressions are as exact and as fast as a hand pulling away from a hot stove.

BEWARE OF BLIND SPOTS

Sound defensive driving not only demands the proper reaction between full vision and the reflexes, but also a thorough knowledge of the built-in blocks to vision in all cars. These are the blind, or blacked-out areas, caused by the structure of the car. An awareness and absolute respect for the danger that lies in these specific cones of blindness that surround an operator as he speeds along the highways is the best tool that a defensive driver has at his command.

The blind areas in a car are located wherever the metal structure breaks the vision in front, to the side, or behind. The rear left and right flanks are the worst blind areas. Objects hovering at these areas of the car cannot be seen through the rear-view mirror. *You must glance over your shoulder.*

On the left, for instance, an approaching car could have its right bumper abreast of your front door handle and you would still not know it was there without turning to look. Many accidents occur under these circumstances, when a driver pulls out without turning to look. In this sense, a blind faith in mirrors is downright dangerous.

There are even larger blind areas to the right rear. Even a large truck or bus could be hidden by them. Glance to the right and far enough back before moving over into a right lane.

Most drivers have a natural fear of looking away from the road ahead to perform this lifesaving craning operation. But be assured that in the time it takes to turn your head to the rear for a check to right or left, a car going 30 miles an hour will travel a distance equal to only its own length. And, as sound defensive driving practice dictates, no car should ever be traveling at that speed within a car's length of a vehicle in front under any normal circumstances.

This situation involves the two most common causes of highway accidents: following too closely is the first and moving into another traffic lane without looking to the rear is the second.

There are emergencies when we are instinctively prompted to swerve suddenly into another lane. Never yield to this temptation unless you have time to check over your shoulder, or unless catastrophe lies surely and directly ahead.

FOR SOUND DEFENSIVE DRIVING

By knowing the blind areas of his own car the defensive driver will take the next mental step in sound defensive driving procedure and become accustomed to the blind areas surrounding other drivers. He will be conditioned to respond to the potential danger that exists when he is moving through the blind areas of the car ahead or to the side. He will be prepared by habit—and in advance—for a defensive maneuver: braking back or honking, or whatever is necessary in the situation. A defensive driver will not hover at the rear corners of other vehicles. If traffic forces him to be there, he will be ready with some form of defensive action should the other vehicle swerve into his lane.

*The best advice at all times is to stay where your car can be seen, or back far enough to allow time for braking.*

In addition to blind spots, the greatest single impairment to effective vision on the road is darkness. Our field of vision is narrowed fantastically at nighttime. During the hours of darkness, a driver can see only one-tenth of what he can see in the daylight. At night, the pupil of the eye dilates, causing a distorted image. Objects and cars seem much closer than they really are, depending on how much the pupil has dilated and how dark the night.

Another defensive driving practice is to keep your speed low enough to account for reduced forward vision depending on the range of your headlights. While it is better also to watch the tail lights of the vehicle ahead as a guide for your path than stare at oncoming lights in the other lane, the best idea is to look ahead for any illumination that could aid your depth perception. All these considerations fall under the proper use of vision, a respect for its strengths and weaknesses. This is a cardinal point of sound defensive driving practice.

# CHAPTER 5

# The Nature of the Controls

LEARN BEFORE YOU START

Most beginners are eager to hear the sound of the engine and "get going." They might sit still in the "classroom" for brief discussions of the *natural laws* that govern the behavior of the car, or the *human laws* that govern the behavior of the operator. But by the time the would-be driver is behind the wheel, he wants to prove to himself as soon as possible that he can really drive. This eagerness interferes with his pre-driving indoctrination.

The first thing a good instructor, amateur or professional, should do is calm the beginner and continue to emphasize the nature of the operation he is about to undertake. It is at the beginning when the learner still has a certain degree of healthy respect—not to say, fear—of an automobile, that the facts about the various controls should be discussed. *Many of the worst drivers on the road today are those who jumped into a car, started it up, took their first corner without a collision and never again gave serious thought to the nature of the automobile.*

So the best time to go over the controls with a beginner is

while his willingness to learn is at a peak; that is, before he even starts up the engine. Later on, it may be too late to get him to think about the steering wheel, the accelerator, and the brake. Once he makes actual use of the basic controls, he cannot as a rule be bothered to speculate upon the *correct* use of them.

True, he may not remember everything told him before-hand, but at least he will have been imbued with a curiosity about them that will eventually give more sense and meaning to his driving.

### THE STEERING WHEEL

For instructions concerning the steering wheel, it is helpful to imagine that it is the face of a clock and the driver's hands are the hands of the clock. *In basic position, the left hand should be placed at 10 o'clock and the right hand at 2 o'clock. This produces the most efficient wheel control.*

Turns should always be made from the upper parts of the wheel, for the obvious reason that we can pull down more easily than up. In turning right, both hands should work together on the upper right section of the wheel, reaching hand-over-hand to 1 o'clock and slowly working down to 3 o'clock in a ladder-descending action. In left turns, the same kind of action is performed, starting at 11 o'clock and working down to 9 o'clock.

The steering wheel is one of the most vital parts of the car as far as maintenance is concerned. Many drivers will rush to a repair shop to have an unseemly dent in a fender removed and yet drive for years without paying any attention to a steering wheel that is sluggish or has a dangerous amount of play in it. If the car is in a rest position, you can determine if the wheel is straight by seeing whether the center emblem is upright, or by the position of the spokes.

The average steering wheel can be turned through two complete revolutions, or, in the case of shorter cars, through one and a half revolutions. As a rule, the wheel should not be turned while the car is at rest. It wears out the tires and tends to strain the steering mechanism. But the greatest strain on the steering wheel, of course, comes from taking corners or turns at too high a speed. Any weakness in the apparatus may prove fatal during such stressful maneuvers.

### THE ACCELERATOR

The accelerator, or gas pedal, feeds gas to the engine through the carburetor. The correct placement of the foot is important if the driver is to control the ever-changing flow of gas to the engine.

With an ordinary flat shoe, the entire sole and heel of the foot should rest on the gas pedal, unless the shoe is longer than the gas pedal, in which case the heel should rest on the floor, usually slightly to the left, in a comfortable position. If the shoe has a high heel or spiked heel, only the ball of the foot should engage the gas pedal. The heel may be used as a pivot for leverage from a comfortable position to the left of the gas pedal. One thing to remember: work the pedal with the ball of the foot, not the toes.

Proper use of the gas pedal in conjunction with smooth steering and braking operations offers the best indication of a well-coordinated driver. During straightaway road conditions, the gas pedal is used to regulate speed more generally than the brake. Cutting back on your gas throws the drag of the car against the forward momentum, slowing it, increasing friction, and making control easier. Conversely, stepping on the gas decreases friction, making control of the car in turns more difficult.

It is generally difficult for beginners to find some happy

medium with the gas pedal. They are either "gas happy," feeding the engine more than it can use at a given moment, or hesitant to engage the pedal at all.

In either case, it is necessary to know that the average car, under maximum acceleration, needs about 100 feet to reach a speed of 30 miles an hour. Incidentally, the brake can stop a car going this speed in only 78 feet, confirming that it is more effective for stopping than a mere release of the gas feed.

Another thing the beginner must learn is that maximum acceleration can best be attained by an even, steady increase of pressure on the pedal, not by jamming it to the floor, which floods the engine and diminishes its efficiency in picking up speed.

The same thing applies to a release of the gas pedal. If this is too sudden at high speeds, the engine gets choked, causing an unnatural decrease in speed. Like any other machine, the automobile can be damaged if it is operated incorrectly over a long period of time.

Once the desired acceleration is attained, the car's speed can most economically be sustained by holding the gas pedal one-quarter to one-half the way to the floor.

THE BRAKE

The brake pedal is the most misunderstood control in the car. A little information about the many links in braking apparatus will instill in the driver a respect for the sensitivity of this system.

In the first place, the brake pedal is not connected with the engine in any way except in the case of power brakes which draw their power from there. The braking system is a hydraulic system. A little pressure applied to the pedal is magnified many times on its way to the wheels.

When pressure is applied, fluid is sent from the master

cylinder to each wheel cylinder, where the braking effect takes place. There is an external contracting band made of flexible steel fastened to each backing plate. When the hydraulic pressure of the braking system forces the band to contract, an inner lining is placed into frictional contact with the outside face of the friction drum on the wheels, causing the braking action.

*In a sense, both the brake and the gas pedal are feeding fluids to the car, so they both demand the same kind of careful, well-modulated pressure for most effective use, except, of course, in emergencies.*

The ball of the right foot should be placed on the brake, in an angular position with the toes pointed to the right. To get the proper leverage, one must brace oneself against the door with the left side of the body with the legs apart and the weight of the body resting mainly on the left buttock. The right knee should be tilted toward the right side of the car during full braking action.

Many drivers hesitate to engage in the slight distortion of the most attractive posture in order to brake properly. This is particularly true of women drivers. But they should place sound driving procedure above any desire to maintain a "ladylike" position behind the wheel.

Most new drivers start the braking process too late or continue it too long. In the latter instance, the car will pitch and jerk if pronounced pressure is applied after the car is sufficiently slowed to stop. By using the ball of the foot, a driver can learn to sense when the car has received enough braking pressure and to ease his foot on the brake so as to come to a smooth stop. Admittedly, the knack for this takes time to acquire. If you give more thought to slowing the car rather than stopping it, you will learn more quickly. Try to stop at least a car's length from the point where the car must come to rest and then inch up toward the intended position.

Slamming on the brakes at high speed causes a locking

action that breaks the car's friction and dangerously reduces control. Avoid braking through curves, on downgrades, and across railroad tracks. Slow the vehicle as you approach these and use slight acceleration to maintain maximum control. Pumping the brakes is necessary only when you have to stop suddenly, on icy or wet streets, or when traveling at 50 miles an hour or faster.

The tricky thing about using the brake is that a swift movement to pedal must be followed by slow, well-modulated application of pressure. This demands well-trained reflexes and good natural coordination.

Remember, when you apply a brake too suddenly, rear traffic is afforded little reaction time. A good defensive driver would be as cautious about jamming on his brakes without checking what is behind him as he would be about changing lanes without turning his head to survey the blind spots.

### EMERGENCY BRAKE

This is the pedal or lever that protrudes from under the dashboard, usually to the left of the steering wheel. The emergency brake is connected to the rear wheels only, by means of cables. The emergency brake should always be on when a car with automatic controls is in the NEUTRAL position but it does not have to be used when the gear is in PARK position, unless the vehicle is on an incline, since PARK locks the transmission so the rear wheels cannot turn anyway.

### THE HORN

The horn is the most overused and greatly abused control on any car. It would be interesting to see whether safety on the highways would not actually be improved by doing away with car horns. This may seem a bit extreme, but there is reason to believe that if drivers concentrated more on effective defensive maneuvers than on horn-honking, there would be fewer accidents and fewer deaths.

Except in areas where the law against unnecessary horn-blowing is enforced, horn-blowers have a way of flooding areas of congestion with a dangerous atmosphere of emergency and tension.

A horn-honker can startle the daylights out of a driver who is concentrating on his driving problems. It sets up a circuit of irritation that runs like electricity through a segment of traffic, throwing even good drivers off their best form and plunging poor or new drivers into a state of dangerous panic.

A good defensive driver, having already weighed the psychology of the horn-honker, will resist the impulse to get angry and answer in kind or to become rattled. For his own part, a defensive driver has realized, again in advance, that using the horn—except in rare instances—does no good and constitutes a road hazard to other drivers.

Horns have been so overused that they have lost most of their effectiveness as warning signals even in real emergencies, like the shouts of the boy who cried "Wolf!" But there are times when it must be used—for instance, as a warning to a car ahead when you cannot stop in time. When passing in the daytime, tap the horn lightly if a warning seems necessary. At night, it is better to flicker your lights.

Excessive horn-honking, while it may seem only an irritating symptom of a motoring age, actually exposes a much deeper and more dangerous fallacy on the part of most drivers. The horn-honker is saying, in effect, "Look out, here I come." This means that the driver is depending on others to take caution against any mishap he might precipitate. It is this pervasive kind of thinking—that the other fellow will somehow make sure there is no accident—that lies behind an incredibly high percentage of mishaps on the roads today.

A defensive driver thinks in the opposite way. He assumes that he and he alone can prevent an accident. If he leaves the matter to chance, as millions of drivers do every day, then the odds run heavily against his safety.

## THE MIRROR

Other than the horn, mirrors are the most thoroughly misunderstood and misused appliances on cars. If the mirrors were removed from training cars, drivers could be trained to realize that their own eyes are by far the best safety device at their disposal.

Mirrors at best offer only fragmentary reflections. They can become misaligned, and most important of all, they cannot inform you about what is happening at the blind spots of your car.

Any car you can see in the rear-view mirror is probably no threat to you. Unless it is following too closely, it can stop in time or otherwise adjust to any change in your direction. But what about the car approaching or hovering within the dangerous rear blind areas? Your rear-view mirror is no help at all in keeping track of these. The average motorist tends to rely too heavily upon the mirror, which gives him a false sense of security that often proves fatal. The mirror should be used only for a general view or for stopping without changing lanes. Whenever possible, look behind you before changing directions.

## DIRECTIONAL OR HAND SIGNALS

The most common error in the use of signals, whether automatic or by hand, is that they are not made in time. To allow enough reaction time, the turn signal must be given well in advance. The most common error is to stick out the hand or throw the signal gear after the turn is already begun. By this time, the car's position makes any signal seem superfluous, not to say ridiculous.

How far from the point of turn the signals should be made

depends on the speed of the traffic. Before the foot leaves the gas pedal and usually a half-block advance warning in the city and a block or more on the highway will do. The lever for signaling a turn is, of course, on the underside of the steering wheel. If you remember "upright," you will not forget that the gear is pushed up for a right turn and down for a left turn.

Many situations occur in which a hand signal is much safer than an automatic signal and a few situations in which hand signals are an absolute must. As a rule, cars produced later than 1956 carry larger-sized signal lights, which do the job under most circumstances—if, that is, they are free from dust or snow and not washed out by sun glare.

However, hand signals should be used in daylight when stopping to park or when pulling away from the curb. This "must" often stumps beginners in a driving test. Another instance in which a hand signal is absolutely essential is during sudden stops. This signal must be given whenever possible at least 50 feet in advance. With bad road conditions, brakes should be pumped for some distance prior to a stop. When slowing to a stop or to park, wave traffic around your car.

AUTOMATIC CONTROLS

The fundamental gauges and devices for automatic controls differ just as cars do. These should be explained to you by a car salesman, mechanic, or instructor. The main controls, such as the brake, the accelerator, and the steering wheel are in the same place in all American cars; so if you can master one car you can drive them all, although the "feel" is different.

P—PARK—is not on all cars. It combines the role of NEUTRAL and the emergency brake. Later models will start in this position. PARK locks the transmission so the rear wheels cannot turn.

R—REVERSE—is of course, for backing. It can also sometimes be used in place of PARK.

N—NEUTRAL—is for starting or parking but must always be used with the emergency brake.

D—DRIVE—is for going forward.

L—LOW—is for extra pull or less engine compression.

A *passing gear* has been added to the transmission of many new cars. This enables one to gain an extra ten to twenty miles of speed for passing purposes. When using this gear, push the gas pedal all the way to the floor and hold for a second.

A good defensive driver should have a thorough intellectual grasp of how the controls work. He should know the dashboard panel as well as a pilot knows his, before he actually begins to use these in driving situations.

# CHAPTER 6

# Taking Over the Controls

## COMMON PROBLEMS

Every beginning driver has special problems that are peculiar to him, but all share, to some degree, certain common difficulties. The most prevalent are mistaking the gas pedal for the brake; confusing directions, especially in backing; using an incorrect signal; accelerating too fast; braking too hard or riding the brake; and gripping the wheel tensely and looking too close at the front end of the car or the road surface immediately ahead.

Almost all new drivers have an unreasonable fear of oncoming cars that are safely out of the path of their vehicle. They are also inclined to keep long distances between their car and a vehicle in front or behind. The beginning driver should be taught not to respond to false dangers. For example, if the car is traveling 30 miles an hour, he should learn not to use the brake unless another vehicle ahead falls back to within three car lengths, a safe following distance.

Beginners are apt to commit the dangerous folly of maintaining full acceleration through a moving turn. The car should be braked well in advance of the turn; and once the car is slowed, *the brake should be held until the car is aimed well into the path of the turn.* Remember: the slower the speed, the greater the degree of control.

When turning from a dead stop, the acceleration, of course, has to be increased, but it should remain slight until the car has completed the turn. The new driver also has to be on guard against not turning the wheel too slightly, too slowly, or moving the car too fast and against holding through the turn too long. The beginning driver also has trouble, when his hands and mind are preoccupied with a turning maneuver, resuming acceleration in time.

Knowledge of these common difficulties will prevent the beginning driver from becoming too impatient with himself when he first confronts them. An awareness of them is also helpful to anyone teaching a prospective driver. Once they have been considered, the beginner should be afforded his first actual run-through at the controls of the automobile.

POSTURE

After adjusting the car seat, sit to the extreme left. Though it may seem unnatural at first, the body should be left of the steering wheel center, against the door at a slightly angular position. *Only a proper sitting position can assure proper vision and braking leverage.*

STARTING THE CAR

Automatics can be started in N or P only. Before turning on the key, press gas pedal to the floorboard and release to set the automatic choke. If the automatic has been broken in properly, the car will start without pressure on the gas pedal. Be sure to keep your foot on or over the brake.

All cars need a 60-second warm-up period. In cold weather, this period should be increased to several minutes.

Here are the simple starting steps:
1. Place gear lever at N or P.
2. Turn the ignition to start—and release.
3. Hold brake and change gear lever to D.
4. Release emergency brake.
5. Check side and rear traffic.
6. Signal and proceed.

Do not rely on mirrors for your traffic checks. Turn your head to scan the blind spots. Use a hand signal in the day-time, a directional signal at night. Proceed only when assured that all is clear. Apply the gas gradually, but withhold full acceleration until you have checked the traffic ahead. The car in front of you should be far enough away so that you can see its tires on the road. Proceed to normal acceleration.

**STOPPING**

Stops at all stop signs or signal lights do not require hand signals unless the stop is sudden. Ordinarily, brake lights serve as sufficient warning. You should begin stops at high stop signs or stop lights while far enough behind the car ahead to see its tires on the paving. You should aim to stop a full car length behind the vehicle ahead and allow your car to creep forward until the bumper of the car ahead drops from view. Ideally, there should be at least 6 feet between your bumper and the rear bumper of the car ahead. This will appear to be about 4 feet from the vantage point behind the wheel. When stopping in heavy lines of traffic, hand signals should be used because brake lights fall into blind areas in close traffic. The latter fact accounts for most of the rear-end collisions we see on almost any Sunday or holiday when traffic is dense.

Here are the stopping steps:
1. Check rear-view mirror.
2. Give hand signal if called for.

3. Ease off the gas pedal gradually.

4. Brake gradually, easing up as car slows.

Anyone teaching a beginner may have occasion to notice that he will unconsciously pull to one side as he slows down. As we have said, the hands on the wheel automatically follow the visual impulse to either side. *Here, again, you will see evidence of the way the muscles tend to direct the car where the driver is looking,* though in this case the beginner may be gripping the wheel too tightly.

PULLING IN CLOSE TO THE CURB

This is one of the most challenging tests of a driver's co-ordination. It can only be mastered with surety after many of the basic driving functions become second nature. For just this reason, aligning close to the curb is a key problem in virtually all driving tests, one incidentally which causes many failures. It can only be accomplished consistently after many other basic driving functions are mastered. Many drivers never learn how to pull close to the curb correctly. Doing this should be faced as soon as possible.

When a standard auto is close to the curb, there is a blind spot to the right extending forward 12 to 18 feet. Pulling close to the curb is one maneuver that justifies looking closely, unless the fringe is very highly developed.

There is a rule of thumb for telling whether or not you are close enough to the curb. As you pull in to the curb, you will see it emerge from the blind spot into view ahead of you. If the curb appears to stretch before you at a point somewhat *to the left* of the hood center line, the car is within the pre-scribed 6 inches to 1 foot distance of the curb. If, on the other hand, the curb seems to be extending ahead at a point to the *right* of the hood center line, then the car is too far away from the curb. This check holds only when the driver is sitting properly to the left of the wheel. The rule applies to the average car on streets that are not excessively sloped and when the curb is of average height.

In cars made before 1958, the driver can use the tail light of a vehicle parked for a similar guide. When the left head-light is aligned with the left tail light, your car will be about as far away from the curb as the one ahead. But some later, full-size standard models do not have their lights placed where they can be used in this way.

When pulling away from a curb, remember to use a hand signal in daylight, even after you have checked with the rear-view mirror and turned to scan blind spots. These multiple measures are not only a matter of good driving habit, but there is always a chance you might have missed something coming from behind while concentrating on the controls for turning out.

BACKING STRAIGHT

This is another basic maneuver that sometimes thwarts novices during driving tests. Here, again, the most common error is to look to the side, usually to the right rear fender, causing the turning impulse to follow suit unwittingly.

Actually, there is no simpler maneuver than backing straight, if the driver maintains a proper body position and correct eye projection. Having shifted into reverse with the foot on the brake, he should turn sideways, with his back braced against the door, gripping the seat with the right hand and holding the left hand in a natural position toward the top of the wheel.

For correct eye focus, choose a place or object a half block away at the center of the desired path behind. If both the car and wheel are straight, there should be no need for wheel movement, unless the road is sharply banked and makes compensating adjustments necessary.

A word of caution: There should be no unnecessary glances

forward while backing. There is a natural tendency to do this, arising from uncertainty. It is so much wasted motion and obviously a dangerous practice as well. In backing, many experienced drivers rely on the rear-view mirror. This is also a mistake because the blind spots are not exposed. Another common error is to look over the left shoulder or out of the left window or door. All these actions make it impossible to keep track of the hazards on the right. Always look straight back over the *right* shoulder and back slowly.

# CHAPTER 7

# Turns and Parking

## TURNS

### LET YOUR EYES LEAD YOU

The greatest aid in learning to make correct turns is a thoroughly trained and confident skill in seeing correctly. The beginning driver's fears force his vision to work close and downward toward the path of the car. The only way to help him overcome these fears is to train the driver to look up and out in the intended direction of his vehicle. Only in this way can he gain confidence that his car will most naturally follow the focus of his sight.

Until this ability to scan away from the hood is attained, turns will be the source of greatest difficulty for the new driver. Even on a straightaway, following the center of the hood with the eyes prevents safe viewing of what is ahead. The same practice in a turn is even more troublesome because it disregards the destination of the vehicle. Incorrect use of the vision through turns sets up a running conflict between the driver's intended direction and his muscular reflexes, which automatically respond to where he is looking. So it is an absolute must that the student learn to look up and out to the center of the path the car will take, once the turn is completed.

The beginner's reflexes are slow to respond to the fact that much less gas is needed in a turn than on a straightaway. He is also reluctant to change the path of the car, because his notion of safety has been attuned to traveling in a straight line. As a result, first turns are usually made with too much gas and too little turning. The novice should be reminded that the steering wheel and not the gas pedal changes the direction of the vehicle.

Of course, the trick is to coordinate through sharp judgment the degree of the turn with the amount of gas. This is for some students as difficult as rubbing the head and patting the stomach at the same time. He also soon learns that there may be a different "feel" for turning every corner. Even when the corner is "uniform," he may encounter some existing condition that calls for refinements in his reactions. A sense of panic seizes the new driver during his first turns. If he is exposed to improper instruction from the beginning, this phobia is apt to become a lifelong fixation. The student balks at throwing the wheel far enough into a turn because he is afraid he will have to fight the vehicle to get it back into a straight driving position. His fears, however, reverse the real situation. Actually, the only fight he might have with the car results from turning too slowly or holding through the turn too long.

*This again comes—and we cannot emphasize this often enough—from looking along the path of the turn, rather than up and out to the center of the path the car will travel once the turn is achieved.*

The beginner is also distracted by any close moving or stationary objects once he places his car into a turn. This is also due to a lack of confidence in his driving eye. Here he is called upon to gauge relative distances, most often between two moving vehicles, rather than the absolute relationship between his moving vehicle and the center line of a highway or a "fixed" line of traffic coming toward him. Here he can see again that only the habit, and the refined judgment that results from it, of looking up and out can help him through the complexities of turning situations.

*The beginning driver must undo or, if you will, unlearn his habit of looking down and close. Were this mastered, turns would be only slightly more difficult than driving in a straight line.*

Furthermore, beginning drivers instinctively sense that turns are a great challenge to their rudimentary skills. They tend to become slightly hysterical while making them, further "jamming" the reflexive relationship between the eye's aim and the automatic tendency of the muscles to steer the car to follow it. Therefore, proper instruction should deal realistically with the requirements of a turn but without over-dramatization.

### HAND-OVER-HAND TECHNIQUE

In normal driving, the hands are kept at 10 and 2 o'clock for maximum control. But in turns, when more than half a turn of the steering wheel is needed, a so-called hand-over-hand technique is called into play. This is the ladder-climbing action described earlier, when the wheel is pulled with an alternating application of both hands, from 11 o'clock down to 9 o'clock on left turns and from 1 to 3 o'clock on right turns. The hand-over-hand technique demands that both hands be 6 inches apart when engaging the wheel, since leverage goes as one hand pulls the wheel downward beyond the halfway mark and the other hand should be ready to take over at the top of the wheel.

Statistics show that no corner can be taken with safety at more than 12 miles an hour. Students have trouble with turns during driving tests at even 8 miles an hour. Of course, during periods of rush-hour congestion, a policeman will wave vehicles through turns as quickly as possible; so there is no absolute rule to cover all contingencies.

Specifically, there are two basic kinds of turns—coordinated turns and square turns. Coordinated turns are made when there is plenty of space. Square turns are executed when space is limited. There are many turns, however, that may incorporate characteristics of both coordinated and square turns.

COORDINATED TURNS

These are made at curves in the highways or at urban intersections where there is considerable space, or when a tighter, square turn is impossible. For all turns, a driver should maneuver his car into the proper lane at least half a block in advance of the point of turn and even as much as two blocks in advance in heavy traffic.

To emphasize a point of caution, never proceed with a plan to turn unless the car is in the right lane or position at least 100 feet (or 5 car-lengths) before the point of turn. *Even more important, try not to leave room between your vehicle and the direction you plan to turn. When you do, you will be turning into a path of potential collision.*

In coordinated turns, the eye, judgment, and muscular responses of both the arms and legs must exchange messages more rapidly than an IBM computor. The best approach, as we have indicated for all driving procedures, is to emphasize the rational or intellectual components of the maneuver first, since more than automatic muscular responses are directly involved. During turns, the mind must actively arbitrate the other centers of response at all times. There is no better way to get it to do this than to train the student from the beginning to conceive of this kind of complex maneuver in intellectual terms, and then proceed.

One of the basic premises of defensive driving is that

without proper prior indoctrination, faulty habits of the re-flexes will set in and be hard to undo.

Here is the general procedure for left turns:

1. Signal for a left turn, check rear-view mirror, glance to blind spots, and maneuver the car slowly toward the center line. In heavy traffic, the driver must position his car two blocks in advance.

2. As you approach the turn, slow to 10 miles an hour. Check the traffic again, to the left, to the right, oncoming, and again in the rear-view mirror.

3. By looking through the left front window into the street you are about to enter, you will receive an impulse as to when to start the turn. Left turns should be aimed at the portion of the right lane you are entering nearest the center line. In a four-lane street, the turn should be made into the lane nearest the center line. Through the turn, continue to look along the channel where the turn should be completed and you will receive another impulse informing you when to allow the steering wheel to spin back to its normal position.

4. Having completed the turn, proceed for a few seconds and then, after signals and checks for a move right, maneuver the car slowly to the right of the street and resume normal driving.

Here is the general procedure for right turns:

1. Signal for a right turn, check rear-view mirror, glance at blind spot, and maneuver to the right within two or three feet of the curb.

2. Again checking conditions, slow to 5 miles an hour.

3. Right turns should be made tight into the right channel of the street you are entering. Look beyond the point where your turn should bring you and your impulses will dictate when you have turned far enough and when to release the wheel, as in left turns.

*Again, remember: in any kind of turn, the car will tend to follow your eyes. So look beyond the point where the turn*

*will bring you and not straight ahead at each point in the
turn. In other words, let the turn follow your eyes and not
the other way around.*

Many drivers turn too slowly or too little and have to fight
the wheel to get themselves to the point where the turn should
have brought them. This will not be necessary if the operator
"looks" correctly.

SQUARE TURNS

These are made when space is limited or the car is at rest
at a point of turn.

Here is the procedure for a left square turn:

1. Signal and check as for a coordinated left turn.

2. Then approach until the front bumper is lined up with
the center line of the street you are entering. Turn the wheel
rapidly, using only slight gas or the car's momentum if it is
sufficient. Find a fixed point in the center of the street you
are entering, possibly a signal light or a stop sign a block
ahead. Again, the direction of your gaze will trigger off the
impulse to turn and then to release the wheel so it can spin
back in place through the palms of your hands.

If an oncoming vehicle indicates that it also is about to
make a left turn across your path, never approach beyond the
point where that car's tires can be seen on the paving.

Here is the procedure for a right square turn:

1. Slow down, signal, and check as for left turns.

2. Line up the front bumper with the curb of the street
you will enter. When aligned, the front end will appear to
be a fender length beyond, and can be seen through the extreme right side of the windshield.

3. Move slowly as you turn the wheel rapidly all the way
to the right.

4. If the vision is used correctly, the impulse to release

the wheel will come when the vehicle is about 45 degrees through the turn. Here is where many make a mistake. At this point, some drivers, almost always beginners, look away from the distant directional reference point. It appears that the car is not headed properly, so they look down to "study" the situation. This results in the turn being held beyond the required 90 degrees and a fight with the wheel ensues. The impulse to release the wheel at the proper halfway point through a square right turn will come naturally if the eyes remain on a distant fixed point along the intended path.

Because of the difficulty in looking away from the hood to the car's intended goal, an inexperienced driver should not execute turns except under the supervision of an instructor. The instructor can tell by watching the beginner's eyes whether to make the turn himself should the novice be responding improperly.

Many drivers tend to swing too far out on a turn, to make them at too wide an angle. This tendency stems from a fear of coming too close to a curb, for instance, on a right turn. They are also reluctant to alter the direction of the car from a straightforward movement, since, as we have said, safety is associated with holding the vehicle in a straight line. Many drivers worry about the back end of the car while turning. But an automobile is not a trolley car. There is no need to worry about the swing of the rear end of an automobile since it follows the same track as the front end, as long as it is lined up correctly.

It is worth repeating that turns engage a subtle interplay of judgment, vision, and muscular reflexes. The beginner should be warned about holding the turn after acceleration has been resumed. Although we have pointed out that braking should precede the start of the turn, at first the brake should be engaged throughout the turn with slight pressure to steadily control the speed necessary to carry through a turn; or, to put it another way, to help keep the turn "tight."

## PARKING

Parking problems, like turning problems, often prove stumbling blocks on driving exams. The most troublesome aspect of parking in general is that it calls for "close-in" work with the eyes and this tends to interfere with the most effective driving vision.

### HEAD-IN PARKING

This kind of parking calls for the most room but is relatively simple to do. Follow the pattern of a square turn. Maneuver the car to where the front bumper is abreast or slightly beyond the line of the parking stall. When the bumper is so aligned, from the vantage of the driver's seat, the stall line will appear to intersect the vehicle at the rear of the front fender. This is due to the blind spot between the driver and the actual position of the line in relation to the vehicle.

As we have said, this kind of parking calls for a great deal of room in which to maneuver. So make sure you are placed in position about 20 feet off from the stall you will enter. If you use a distant reference point beyond the center of the stall, your impulse to turn and release will work, as in square turns. The only difference is that you must pull the wheel back to normal when you have held the turn long enough, because the car is slowed to a degree where its momentum is insufficient to spin the wheel back.

In driving cars with automatic controls, no acceleration is needed in the D position to carry through the maneuver. With the earlier manual gear shifts, gas must be applied, but only under the control of the clutch in second gear.

### ANGLE PARKING

Aside from pulling straight into a curb, this is the simplest kind of parking. Use the same techniques employed in coordinated turns. If you keep about 6 feet away from the bumpers of other cars in the line, you will have enough room for this kind of parking. Check and signal as for any change in direction, and line up with the stall so the right fender appears to be ahead of the nearest side of the angled stall, then turn the wheel quickly but proceed slowly. By looking properly, the impulse to turn the wheel back will come in time to leave you evenly centered in the angled parking stall.

For backing out of angle parking, back out straight for about 4 feet, or until you can see over the trunks of the cars a block away. By the way, a driver never has the right of way when backing. So, having stopped and looked to the rear, back slowly and turn rapidly until the car is in a forward driving position. Once in position, you should shift to DRIVE even before straightening the wheels. If you straighten the wheels before shifting to DRIVE, you may automatically step on the gas when you look up and, of course, the car will still be in reverse. Do not look forward until you have stopped the car and changed the shift.

### PARKING ON A HILL

The basic series of safety steps for parking on a hill involve turning the wheels in toward the curb, setting the shift to N or P, and putting on the emergency brake. The only exception to this is for parking on an upgrade that has a curbing, in which case the wheels are turned outward so the front wheels will swing gently to the curb. If there is no curb, then P and the emergency brake must suffice. If there is no P, then the best thing to do is to shift into the position opposite to the direction that the car might slip. No matter what the circumstances, the car should generally be parked in a manner that would lead it off the road and away from moving traffic should it slip, except in the case of the upgrade with a curb where the wheels are turned out.

To be specific, here are the various parking procedures:

Downgrade with curb: (1) Turn wheel in. (2) Shift to N or P. (3) Set emergency brake. (4) Turn key off. To get away from curb, be sure to back up a couple of feet.

Downgrade without curb: (1) Turn wheel in. (2) Shift to P or R. (3) Set emergency brake. (4) Turn key off.

Upgrade with curb: (1) Turn wheel out and allow car to inch back until the back of right front wheel is lodged gently against the curb. (2) Shift to N or P. (3) Set emergency brake. (4) Turn key off.

Upgrade without curb: (1) Turn wheel in. (2) Shift to P or L. (3) Set emergency brake. (4) Turn key off. Actually the only time the wheels are ever turned out is on an upgrade with a curb. Any other time the wheels should always be turned in since all roads are somewhat sloped. Many drivers do not go along with this, so if you are one of those, at least leave the wheels straight, not turned out.

Caution should be used when allowing the front wheels to "lock" with the curb. If the attack is too abrupt and hard, damage to the tire will result. This is particularly true of tubeless tires, which can be punctured by the action.


PARALLEL PARKING

This maneuver calls for thoroughly developed skills in all the basic driving actions. Any driver who can parallel park consistently well has mastered the mechanical operation of an automobile.

At least 100 feet away from the parking space, the vehicle should be maneuvered to the right so that it will pass parallel to the parking line with at least 2 feet between its right side and the parked cars. This maneuver should be made well in advance, as much as 100 feet or five car lengths from the parking space. Proceed until the steering wheel is abreast of the steering wheel of the car in front of the desired parking place or, if the cars are of different lengths, make sure rear bumpers are even. Once your car is in position, begin to back straight slowly a few feet. Most automatics do not need any acceleration for this kind of backing. They will creep back at the desired rate. After a few feet, turn the wheel rapidly to the right. You should turn so that your position in the driver's seat is abreast of the tail light of the car to your right when the steering wheel has been turned all the way. Another check on whether or not you are entering at the proper 45-degree angle is to look back at the right rear fender. If it appears to be headed straight for the curb, then you are in the correct position at the point that your steering wheel is abreast of the left tail light of the car on your right. Another check at this point is to look over the left shoulder through the small left rear window on the left rear side. If the left front fender headlight of the car behind you can be seen, your vehicle is at the correct 45-degree angle. Now let the car back about a foot farther, and turn all the way to the left twice as fast as the original turn of the wheel to the right. Ideally, if the turn is done properly the car should slide in close to the curb (closer than 6 inches). If the vehicle is too far out, the final backing phase was too slow; if the tire rubs the curb, the final backing was too sudden, the turning too slow. If the back end is out from the curb, the turn was too fast in relation to the backing. In the latter, shift to D and inch forward, turning to the right until the vehicle is properly aligned.

Now let's go over the parallel parking procedure step by step:

1. Line up 100 feet in advance.

2. Check mirror, give hand signal 50 feet in advance.

3. Align steering wheel with that of car directly in front of the space you intend to use.

4. Start backing slowly, and when your steering wheel is even with the other car's front-door handle (the back-door handle if your car has power steering), turn wheel quickly to

the right. Stop and check: steering wheel should now be in line with tail light of other car.

5. Now move slowly on back until the vehicle assumes a 45-degree angle; your right fender should appear to be headed directly for the curb.

6. Start the car moving again—but very slowly, and turn the wheel all the way to the left, faster than before since there is twice as much turning to do. Roads are sloped and the car tends to move faster, so be sure to control it with the brake.

7. Once you have slithered in along the curb, inch forward, turning fast to the right until the car appears to be straight.

To get out of a parallel parking space, shift to reverse, turn wheel to the right, backing the car gently until it touches the curb. The car is now angled for a turn out. Shift to drive, turn wheel rapidly to the left, inching forward. Do not attempt to straighten the wheel or apply gas until the vehicle is again on a 45-degree angle.

Now, step by step, let's go over the getting out procedures:

1. Reverse slowly, turning wheel to the right.

2. Shift to D, creep forward, turning rapidly all the way to the left.

3. Check mirror, give signal, and look over left shoulder to check rear traffic. Do not straighten wheels until car reaches a 45-degree angle.

*Some Safety Tips:* Having discussed the various basic driving maneuvers, let us end this phase of instruction with a review of some basic safety measures touched on throughout:

1. When in doubt, new drivers should put their foot on the brake, then do their thinking.

2. Never stare out of your path while car is in motion; just glance.

3. Develop fast movements to and from the gas pedals, but press pedals easily.

4. Do not use the horn in place of the brake.

5. Never turn the wheel while the car is standing still; it is hard on you and the car.

6. Stop a car length in advance, then creep up to where you should be.

7. Do not automatically swerve from an animal in your path; their instinct is better than ours.

# CHAPTER 8

# Ownership and Maintenance

## THE REAL PRICE

While the new formal emphasis on driving in the curricula of the nation's high schools means that the new generation of drivers will probably be more safety-conscious than the previous, it has also brought its own set of new problems.

Owning a car has become more than the fad it used to be in the schools. It is now something of a must in many communities. Most high schools were planned with only limited parking space. Now the need for greater parking areas has taken its place with the need for more athletic facilities and classrooms as one of the regular questions facing school boards throughout the country.

Also, now that driving has been placed in the category of an academic pursuit, youngsters have a persuasive argument for owning a car. Parents who in the past might have successfully resisted the high school senior's pleas for an automobile, do so now at the risk of the charge of interfering with the advancement of his education. While this is something of an exaggeration, it is true that students can make a better case for having their own car than ever before.

In any event, more and more students have their own cars at an earlier age than in the past. As we have said, this may result eventually in their becoming more responsible drivers than their parents ever were. But it has also brought new friction into the home as to how the car is to be paid for and maintained. For the truth is that most students—and their parents—have a highly unrealistic idea of how much money is needed to make a car a functional part of a person's everyday life.

The initial cost of purchasing a car, especially when broken down into weekly payments, can be quite misleading. The high school senior who spots a nifty two-tone number in the local used-car lot buys the car without any real idea of how much it will cost to own and operate it. There is the classic story of the student who bought a car to help with his driving courses but found the upkeep so costly that he quit school altogether in order to meet the payments and expenses.

Decades ago, the mechanically inclined youngster bought needed parts with his allowance and assembled a car and somehow managed to keep it going on pin money; but those days are gone forever. And while it is true that you can still see the sale signs in used-car lots, "$10 down," owning a car today, even an old one, presents budgetary demands that the average student is not equipped to meet. This has brought about minor crises in many families. Though decisions are usually readily worked out, it is easier on everyone if the economics of car ownership are dealt with before the student and parents acquire a "bargain" car that is more than they bargained for.

The cost of maintenance alone for even a brand-new car is at least $50, and probably more, for the first year. The cost doubles the second year, and triples the third. From the fourth year, the upkeep will be at least $200. This, of course, does not include the formidably high insurance costs and various miscellaneous expenses. Here is an approximate breakdown of costs for a new car for one year. The figures are rough minimums, applied to 10,000 miles of driving in one year.

| | |
|---|---|
| Lubrication every 1,000 miles | $15 |
| Oil changes and oil filters | 18 |
| Brake adjustments, plus fluids | 7 |
| Gas and oil | 260 |
| Insurance | 100 |
| Car registration, license plates and driver's license | 20 |
| Miscellaneous | 80 |
| TOTAL | $500 |

If your car is over two years old and you can keep costs down to $500, then there is something unusual about you as a driver or about your car. Among the miscellaneous expenses mentioned above, we could include over-all repairs and adjustments, tires, brake linings, pumps and hoses, fan belts, tune-ups, points and spark plugs, not to mention the replacement of any major parts that surely will be needed; so the estimated costs are minimal.

CAR INSURANCE

For a subject that is as basically simple as car insurance, there are an amazing number of drivers who never do seem to learn what it is all about. The purchase price of a new car may include the cost of a collision insurance policy, which is carried in the monthly payments. But collision insurance covers only your own car in accidents involving damage of more than $50. Liability insurance, on the other hand, pays for the injuries or damage that your driving may cause. There was a time when a $5,000-10,000 policy was considered sufficient. But legal claims by contending drivers now have soared to the point where $25,000-50,000 coverage is generally recommended for real protection. The greater the amount of the policy, the lower the premium for each $1,000 of coverage. A comprehensive policy, in addition to liability, includes insurance against vandalism, fire, theft, or storm damage to your vehicle.

Insurance companies charge a higher rate for men between the ages of 16 and 25 and are generally considering a rise in the rates for women between the ages of 29 and 40. Statistics show that these sex-age groups are involved in more accidents than other comparable groups. This has been attributed to the high degree of vitality that causes persons in these sex-age brackets to drive more exuberantly than others. Then too, they comprise 48% of the drivers on the roads.

MAINTENANCE

It is a basic tenet of sound defensive driving that a great deal of care should be used to make sure that the vehicle is in safe and sound working order. Unfortunately, most drivers pay more attention to the outward appearance of their car than to the interior workings. One reason for this is an honest but nonetheless deplorable ignorance concerning the symptoms of mechanical troubles.

The only two gauges that should go past "the halfway mark" of their dials are, of course, the fuel and the amperage, which throbs past that mark to show the battery and generator are in good working order. If the temperature gauge goes over the mark, it may indicate serious trouble in the car's cooling and circulatory system. A check-up should tell.

There are a variety of troubles that can occur in the complex linkage of the steering mechanism. If the car steers stubbornly, it could be something as simple as too little air in the tires. Steering that is "too easy" could indicate loose linkage. If you can turn the wheel as much as two inches without engaging the front wheels, there is too much "play." This should be attended to immediately by a good mechanic.

If the brakes feel "spongy" or give too far toward the floor, the hydraulic system should be checked for leaks. Your life may depend on this particular safety precaution.

Drivers are especially careless about alignment. If a car pulls to one side, the cause may be a leaking wheel cylinder or too tight an adjustment of the wheels. More than likely, however, the wheels should be aligned. Most drivers put this off for reasons of economy. In the meantime, it costs them more in wear and tear on tires than the alignment would in the first place. One way, of course, of determining whether the wheels are aligned is to drive down a flat and empty road with hands off the wheel. If the car pulls to the side, the car may be beset with one of the above-mentioned troubles.

If the car seems to lope when at moderate or full speed, the points or spark plugs may be worn or faulty. This could also be the trouble if the car is hard to start.

Too much heavy smoke from the exahust indicates the car is burning too much oil and may need a ring job. It is impossible to go into everything that might go wrong with a car. There are so many mechanical advances and innovations in the automobile industry today that even skilled mechanics are hard-pressed to keep up with them. A rule of thumb to apply: any irregularity in the tempo or sound of the car's engine or body should be looked into.

*Which Gas?* The variety of sales pitches by the gas and oil companies have thrown the question of what gas or oil to use into a state of utter confusion. One thing you can do is consult the operator's manual dealing with your car. It will provide many useful facts and tell you whether your car is designed for regular or hi-test gas. As a rule, cars with six cylinders, or the less expensive models, function perfectly with regular gasoline, whereas eight-cylinder cars, or the heavier, more expensive models, require gas of higher octane. One test is to try the regular gas. If when depressing the accelerator, a *ping* is produced in the engine, chances are your vehicle needs the hi-test. Detergent gasoline is used to keep the carburetor unclogged. Use of this in most vehicles is optional.

ACCIDENT PROCEDURE

Most drivers have never thought what they would do in case of an accident. This oversight, while natural enough, is due to the faulty thinking discussed earlier: some accidents happen only to "other" people. A defensive driver should be mentally prepared for a course of action in the event of an accident. Even if a driver never has need to put such considerations to the test, a mental run-through will serve to anchor in his mind the fact that he is at all times within a fender's length of an accident.

Here is what to do in case of an accident:

1. Assist the injured, if any. Most persons have a rudimentary knowledge of first aid. This is particularly important for a professional driver or one who spends much time on the road. Give whatever first aid you can.

2. Get help, if required, as soon as possible. In calling the police, indicate whether or not persons have been injured. The information you give the police within the first moments of an accident may spell the difference between life and death for anyone seriously injured. Hail passing cars for assistance, even while the police are en route, to help keep the road clear.

3. When the emergency abates, exchange license numbers, names, addresses, and phone numbers if you are directly involved in the accident. Information about insurance companies should also be noted. If there have been any witnesses, make sure their names are also obtained. Note the hour, weather conditions, position of cars, and all other pertinent

data that may be of use in describing the accident to police and legal authorities.

4. Report the accident to your insurance company; this will assist in determining your liability or that of the other party and also help in settling claims.

ROAD TESTS

Your instructor will know when you are ready to take a road test. He is familiar with what the examiners in your locality will require of you, and will not ask you to submit to an exam until your ability to meet test problems has been demonstrated to his satisfaction and to your own.

Here are some suggestions on how to cope with certain problems that are more or less standard for most tests throughout the country:

1. You should be able to execute left and right turns. An examiner usually calls for a demonstration or six or more of these, to be made as if there were other cars and pedestrians involved. He expects you to turn into a street as if there were a car waiting to come out of it, or to turn out of a street where another car might be waiting to enter. For test purposes, never make any turns at more than 8 miles an hour.

2. Be careful to avoid lines running parallel with your vehicle. Be sure to stop before stop signs and before any crosswalks, sidewalks, or pedestrian paths, even if there are no pedestrians nearby.

3. Be able to demonstrate complete control of the car by executing parallel parking or backing straight. You may also be called upon to make a U-turn or a broken U-turn. The latter is necessary when there is not quite enough room for the U-turn. The car should be maneuvered through the partial U, then backed enough to afford room to achieve the complete change in direction a U-turn would provide.

4. Be able to perform the various parking maneuvers described earlier. Be well versed in the safety cautions for parking on a hill.

5. Be ready for a test of your reaction time. This usually takes the form a sudden stop from a speed of about 20 miles an hour.

6. Be prepared to use hand signals or directional signals. As we have said, hand signals are mandatory for parking or pulling away from the curb. Hand signals in any situation are effective within a wider range than automatic signals in the day time, and in general seem to register sooner. To determine what kind of signal your examiner prefers, ask his opinion on what constitutes the best driving practice.

# CHAPTER 9

# Defensive Driving Applied

## CHECK YOUR ATTITUDE

⟦The elimination of personal fault or human error from driving would save thousands of lives annually.⟧Theoretically, this fact alone should be enough to persuade the motoring public to refine its driving techniques to the point of maximum safety, that is, to adopt a defensive-driving frame of mind.⟧ But, unfortunately, there are many obstacles blocking the way to defensive-driving practice even after the logical advantages of such a method have been conveyed to the car operator.

Earlier, we discussed the lack of a positive attitude as the major bar to the acceptance of the precepts and practices of defensive driving. As you will remember, this attitude is characterized by both fear and arrogance in the many forms they take as harmful influences on our driving.

The arrogant person is reluctant to admit the possibility of personal error, for the psychological reasons suggested earlier. This means that it is impossible for him to imagine self-improvement where it is needed. He is, therefore, not inclined to envision safe-driving precepts. He does not learn from near accidents or errors. Nor does he have a constructive attitude toward the hazards due to the errors of others on the road. He is, as a rule, so bent upon the condemnation of other drivers that he has neither time nor patience to anticipate objectively the threat posed by their faulty driving practices. Needless to say, he has not formulated, nor mentally run through, defensive-driving maneuvers to counter the many ordinary driving errors that threaten his very life every day he steps into his automobile.

A negative attitude is also characterized by the numerous fears we have mentioned. A fearful person is also incapable of assessing the threat from personal error. He might be humble enough to admit fault, but he is in such a state of tension that he cannot do anything about it. The fearful person seldom really learns from his mistakes or refines his driving techniques with an eye to increased safety.

The fearful person is also at the mercy of the driving mistakes of others. Since his mind is constantly distracted from the real problems of driving, he has neither acknowledged the usual threats of personal error that haunt our highways nor conceived and practiced mentally the defensive countermoves that would offset them.

Here are some questions to determine whether or not you have a positive attitude:

1. When stuck behind a road hog, do you seethe with anger and call him names under your breath?

2. Do you blow your horn when other drivers could not even know what you want?

3. Do you antagonize the tailgater in back of you and refuse to let him pass?

4. Do you feel you can be as indifferent as you please as long as you remain within the speed limit and the law?

5. Do you try to be the first one off at a light?

6. Do you try to impress others by showing them how easy driving is for you?

7. Do you feel as if you could never be involved in an accident because you are too good a driver?

8. Do you expect pedestrians and other drivers to watch out for you?

9. Are you the impatient type who hates to wait for anything or anybody?

10. Do you cheat just a little, by breaking laws and reducing the time other drivers will have to react to your moves?

11. Do you feel that you don't have to show others what you are about to do by signals?

12. When another car starts to pass, do you step on the gas?

13. Do you feel that you have to pass everything ahead of you on the road?

14. Do you allow the sense of power that comes with driving to go to your head?

15. When others commit wrongs, do you try to "teach them a lesson"?

16. Do you refuse to help other drivers when they are in difficult spots?

17. Do you race to beat lights or other motorists?

18. Do you feel sure you can stop a car on a dime?

A "yes" answer to any one of these means that your attitude is not completely positive and could spell the difference between life and death under certain circumstances.

So we are reminded that arrogance and fear, both falling under the heading of a negative attitude, or, as already described, the lack of a positive attitude, constitute the single most important problem in an approach to defensive driving. Still another stumbling block to the practice of defensive driving is ignorance of the laws governing our safe conduct on the highways and an enlightened interpretation of them under "existing conditions," that is, conditions that may call for only a conditional adherence to the law, or an actual violation.

Laws, of course, are made to be obeyed, but they cannot

cover every conceivable combination of circumstances that may pertain within the complex traffic patterns of everyday driving. Therefore, there are times when the law is best observed in the breach. The determination of just when the law must be broken in the name of safety will always remain a matter of common sense. But there is little doubt that the adoption of a defensive driving attitude will inspire the driver to view the law within the terms of personal and public safety. First of all, however, he must be well versed in the letter of the law.

It is amazing how many car operators do not know the exact nature of even the most basic traffic regulations. Most drivers never study the traffic regulations of their state after they pass their driving test. Every state publishes its own list of traffic regulations. These may be obtained through the proper state agency to familiarize all drivers with both the old and new regulations governing driving.

The various regulations concerning right of way, or when to yield or not to yield, should be of prime concern. Not only are these questions encountered almost every time we go around the block in a car, they also have figured in more accidents and law cases than any others.

Many of the nuances dealing with such regulations are subtle and admittedly confusing. For instance, most states call it a violation to make a left turn in or out of your own driveway, because such a turn is a hazard in that it impedes two or more lanes of traffic. Virtually every motorist would break such a law; but should an accident follow, the driver who does so would be automatically liable.

Another situation that stumps most motorists arises at an intersection that is not governed by stop lights or stop signs. That there are such intersections is something of an anomaly in this day and age. But they exist and the rule is as follows: it should be regarded as a four-way stop. Approach to a stop and check the other three streets. Any car that has stopped in a position to proceed ahead to you has the right of way.

A driver must yield or stop at all T-streets. A rolling stop must be made at all "yield" signs. If the way is clear, continue through; if not, make a complete stop.

A CAUTION sign always means prepare for a stop and should not be approached at more than 20 miles an hour. Proceed only if the way is clear. People in or near the street should also serve as automatic caution signals.

Red lights, whether flashing or steady, of course, mean stop under any and all circumstances. SLOW indicates caution, with the added warning to clear the intersection. Many drivers, particularly new ones, either want to beat the light or to stop too soon.

When approaching a green light in a 30-mile zone, you should let up on the gas five car lengths (100 feet in advance, giving yourself time to stop should the light turn red, a full car length before any crosswalk. You are automatically in the wrong should you come to rest beyond the proper position for a stop when a light turns red.

Diagonally lined signs (red and white, black and white, or green and white) are reflectors for warnings at night that there is no road beyond, as in the case of a dead-end street, or that the paving narrows or curves dangerously.

In speaking earlier of a judicious interpretation of the regulations, we should have offered school zones as an illustration. Common sense tells us that the signs are up twenty-four hours a day, but that the regulation makes sense only during periods when children are in school. During holidays or before and after school hours, there is no need to creep along as though youngsters were about to run beneath the wheel. There are a number of situations like this in which the law is obeyed only at the expense of common sense. The most important of these has already been mentioned. We are referring to the refusal of many drivers to exceed the speed limit, even though they cause traffic jams and actual pile-ups by not keeping pace with traffic that may be going beyond the speed limit.

Cyclists and pedestrians should be afforded the right of way. Most states have a number of regulations insuring pedestrians the right of way. Even when this is not spelled out, the weight of justice is usually inclined toward the pedestrian; beware when he is about. In any contest with him, let him win. The courts have little sympathy for the driver who hits a person, even if the driver has not broken any regulation.

Many accidents are caused by those who hesitate to act because they are unsure of the laws. Complete familiarity with traffic regulations and their specific applications under existing conditions can offer a defensive driver still another support for his confidence. It will also serve to prepare him for decisive action in tight driving situations where there is no time for memory-searching or speculation.

KNOW CONDITIONS

Besides familiarity with the laws, another aid to sound defensive driving is a knowledge of the unusual conditions that arise from time to time on the road, presenting unfamiliar hazards. Here are some suggestions concerning a few of these:

When crossing railroad tracks, do not rely on automatic signals in the daytime. Hand signal and turn your wheels at a slight angle if the tracks are slippery. Never stop on the tracks. Do not ride across with your foot on the brake. The car should be slowed as you approach and slight acceleration is used. Be sure to glance both ways before crossing.

Avoid puddles and chuck holes like a pox, but not without following sound defensive-driving practices of checks and signals before changing direction to go around them. If you must drive through them, proceed slowly, with only slight acceleration. It is wise to remember that the presence of an obstruction in your path does not give you an automatic legal right to swerve to avoid it.

Any substance between the tires and the paving breaks

the friction and is apt to throw the car out of control. Wet streets are the most common culprit in this respect. Even a thin sheet of moisture can reduce friction 50 per cent. Oil, gravel, dirt, mud, sleet, and ice are worse. Begin a stop far from these hazards wherever possible. The first five minutes of a shower are the most hazardous in driving. The rain forces the usual coat of oil on the road to the surface and it is very dangerous until it is finally washed away as the rain continues.

Skids on slippery surfaces can be eliminated or reduced to safe proportions if anticipated in time. If you approach a slippery area with only the car's slight momentum bearing you along and pump the brakes slightly, you should be able to get by without mishap. But should you find yourself in a skid, the best thing to do is to turn the car in the direction it is sliding. The back wheels are usually doing the sliding because they are not connected with the steering wheel. Turning in the direction of the skid will usually restore control of the car. But many drivers, new ones particularly, cannot think fast enough for this defensive-driving maneuver. The minimal precaution is not to fight the skid but slow as effectively as possible and let it play out.

Contrary to common belief, automatics do not skid as much as vehicles with standard gear shift, and power steering and power brakes are far safer for driving on ice than their manual standard counterparts.

Wet brakes can prove a hazard to both you and other drivers. To avoid wet brakes or "shorting" the car, proceed through watery areas of the road at the lowest speed possible. If your brakes give way because of water exposure, pull to the side of the road and accelerate for several blocks to 15 or 20 miles an hour while "riding" the brakes. This will probably "burn" the brakes dry and is all any mechanic could do for you without replacing parts, which more than likely would not be necessary. Do not "burn" the brake too long, for then an adjustment will be necessary. A word of caution should be said against too much "pumping" of the brakes. This should be done only when you must jolt to a sudden stop or when you are taken by surprise by a slippery area. Too much pumping will impair the hydraulic system and necessitate having it overhauled and the fluid replaced.

Perhaps the most desperate emergency in driving arises when braking power is lost. The thing to do is to pump the foot brake as you grab for the emergency brake. As a last resort, throw gear into reverse.

One misconception that should be put to rest is that a low gear should be used for driving on ice. The low gear is for extra pull or less gas compression. Driving in low under any other circumstances builds up pressure in the transmission, just as racing the engine in PARK would, and can, wreck the transmission. For manual gear shift, the best speed on ice is to start in second and shift back to it before stopping.

### BEWARE OF DANGEROUS DRIVERS

The defensive driver should be on the alert for all abnormal traffic patterns. One that will give him the most trouble is that caused by the road hog. We should learn to live with this kind of highway nuisance. These drivers seem somehow to have been born with the idea that the world belongs exclusively to them. Every road hog has his own particular problem, but their troubles all fall under the heading of indifference or uncertainty. They either straddle two lanes, or slow up the middle lane in heavy, fast-moving traffic. Most of them feel they can drive anywhere and at any pace as long as they stay within the speed limit. These "creepers" simply don't care what happens to anyone else. The best treatment for them is a sound defensive-driving approach that helps you spot them immediately and to steer clear of them. Try to get in front of them if you can; but road hogs can be stubborn in their efforts to thwart you. They usually do this for "moral" reasons, out of some deep sense of scandal at the profligacy of present-day drivers or as a general protest against the fast pace of the age. They are generally pre-occupied with the danger of speed but not with the danger of slowness in fast-moving traffic.

Their opposite number is the speed demon, or the "waltzer and weaver," who rollicks his way through traffic from this lane to that and back again, without signals or checks, as if he were on roller skates. He leaves behind him a wake of panic and resentment. He is of course asking to get hit. He is depending like a child upon the good humor of the fates and the odds of coincidence that will find every driver auto-matically doing everything to make allowances for his devious path, even though he usually cannot be seen until too late. Surely this type of driving represents some form of patholog-ical behavior. We all see it every day. Until law enforcement agencies take fuller account of it and impose heavier penal-ties on this kind of driver, he is bound to persist. So be ready for defensive action to avoid his presence, and be reminded that this variety of road hog places your life in continual jeopardy. You cannot relax your vigilance for a moment. Assume that the speeding road hog is always somewhere nearby.

BE READY FOR ANYTHING

A truly dangerous situation arises when you are changing lanes and, despite all possible checks, are taken by surprise by some car shooting in your path. This may mean that you have allowed too much time to elapse from your check to your move, or it might be simply that your signal was not caught or that some obstruction prevented your seeing some-one else's. In any case, do not follow your first impulse to simply hit the foot brake. This way you might impede traffic in two lanes. The best thing to do is to try to ease yourself back into your former lane. Or if your greatest safety lies in continuing the change, go ahead as fast and precisely as possible—and be ready for anything.

As we have said about drivers who refuse to keep pace with the traffic, creeping is not only a discourtesy but a highly dangerous practice. Don't be a creeper. If you find you are creeping, then you must face the fact that you are frightened, whether you like to admit it or not. You ought to take mental inventory of this fear, try to ferret out the root of it, and master it. The best way to master a fear of keeping pace with the traffic is to keep up with the pack and put your fear to the test of reality. The odds are it will disappear of its own accord.

### SOME COMMON PROBLEMS

In city driving, vision is the main problem. The density of the traffic makes it difficult to see the required city block ahead. The best thing is to keep your vision aimed high ahead in the car's path, scanning through the fringe to the side at all times.

The problems of vision ease somewhat on country roads. The main difficulty here stems from the gravel or sand which reduces friction. Curves are the hazards of the boulevards and call for a change of speed. Another problem is the lack of banking on some of the broad turns. If they are flat or, even worse, slope from the center, then take the turns at slow speed and with caution.

The nation's large highways are the scene of most of the accidents that claim lives. This is ironic because, unlike small city streets, they have been constructed especially for the fast-moving, heavy vehicle that is the modern-day automobile. Here is where the public pays the high price for its faulty, nondefensive driving, particularly in its wrong use of vision. The high speeds on the highways leave little time to undo the mistakes that arise from using the eyesight incorrectly, little time to avert the dangers that may lie beyond the limits of too close vision. The greatest danger comes when you are following closely at high speed preparatory to passing. You should be ready at all times for defensive action, should the car ahead of you slow dangerously or change its direction without warning. When approaching a light, even if it is green, let up on the gas a full city block from the intersection. Never stop on a highway. There are times when a driver may be forced to leave the road, to avert a danger in front of or behind him, or for a flat tire. Many drivers have an unrealistic fear of leaving the highway, even when they would apparently encounter no ditches, fences, or obstructions. In most emergencies, off the highway is the safest place you could be, if it can be reached without risking an accident.

Here are some more general defensive-driving do's and don't's:

1. First and foremost, learn to drive scientifically. Train your eyes to look a block ahead and use the fringe vision to watch things to the sides. Take advantage of the full range of your 160-plus-degree field of vision. Learn to trust your reflexes.

2. Don't get hemmed in; always have an alternative path to take.

3. Obey the 3-feet law (except when parking) and stay 3 feet away from parked cars.

4. Keep out of the blind spots of other cars.

5. Stay on the defensive. While driving, always be thinking "what if," and train your mind well in advance to cope with common hazards.

# CHAPTER 10

# Defensive Driving: A Safe Highway to the Future

Fifty years ago when the automobile first made its presence felt upon the American scene, there were starry-eyed predictions concerning the wonderously happy revolution it would bring about in the life of an entire nation. For the most part, this bright prophecy has been more than fulfilled. Man has been marvelously freed from his own slow pace and been given wheels that will carry him swiftly over great distances at a cost that lies within the means of virtually everyone. From the point of view of its impact upon the daily living habits of a whole culture, the automobile may be judged one of the greatest inventions ever conceived by man.

But in the early days of the automobile, no one imagined the carnage that would accompany its benefits. In that same fifty years, probably one million persons have been killed, many millions permanently maimed, and billions upon billions of dollars' worth of property damage has been left in the wake of this single cultural advance. If you telescope the history of the automobile into one imagined picture and place

97

upon the nation's highways every person killed or injured and every wrecked car left by the wayside, you will present your mind with a scene of waste and anguish more terrible than that of any war except World War II. The price we have paid for the common use of the automobile in our daily lives is appalling.

There will always be many people who regard the murderous potentialities of the automobile as inevitable. There will always be those who view the thousands of deaths on the highways every year as the working of fate or the natural consequences of the automobile's function in our lives. But neither of these is true. Obviously, death on the highway is in no sense due to fate; nor is it due to the nature of the machine that man devised to improve the condition of his life. The killer that stalks the highways even during our pleasantest driving hours is human indifference.

The murderer is the collective indifference of the motoring public toward the real cause of death and injury on the highways. It is the personal indifference of the individual operator, multiplied by the millions on the road, that cut down men, women, and children every day, leaving families broken, the dead to be buried, the injured to heal in pain, and the permanently maimed to be cared for by society for the rest of their days. This book was conceived as an attack upon that indifference. It was written out of the conviction that a revolution in the minds of the motoring public could all but eliminate the waste and carnage that has become a grisly concomitant of the automobile age.

As the highways become larger and the cars faster, the need for disciplined driving becomes more and more pressing. The make-do atitude and untrained reflexes of the average motorist are being outstripped by the demand for speed and more speed. The problems of daily driving are already beyond the ingrained habits of thinking and reacting of the average motorist. This book was written to change those thinking habits, to refine those reflexes; in short, to nudge forth the beginnings of a complete intellectual revolution in the approach to driving a car. This approach we have called defensive driving.

A CALL FOR REALISM

The first problem is to present driving as a serious pursuit, something to deal with on a serious and unrelieved intellectual plane. The reasons for this are several. In the first place, it is necessary to expose the common fallacy that driving is as simple and undemanding as riding a bicycle. It is easy to see how this fallacy came to grip the collective mind of the public in the early days. For indeed, many of the first automobiles seemed no more formidable than bicycles with smoky engines attached to four instead of two wheels. The automobile held little menace with its light weight and slow pace. Pedestrians had plenty of time to scamper from its path. For the most part, it was considered a ridiculous indulgence of the rich or a toy for those with a craze for mechanical gadgets. Least of all did it seem the potential menace to public life and limb that it has become in our day and age.

So the first task is to undo the traditional view of the automobile as a mere source of fun and excitement. It may have been that at one time. But today the automobile is no longer the picturesque oddity it once was as it chugged down a country road kicking up comic puffs of dirt along the way. It is no longer the source of quixotic amusement pictured in the silent films, when one and all would step forth from an accident unscathed and ready for more hilarious adventures. This image of the automobile as a slightly zany but absolutely harmless mechanism unfortunately has been handed down from generation to generation almost intact.

And it is a difficult thing to replace this simple-minded picture of the automobile with a realistic one that takes into account its terrifying potentialities for death and destruction. Yet if this national image of the automobile is not radically overhauled, how can you expect the motoring public to be sufficiently impressed with the efforts of the national safety agencies? If a beginning driver climbs into a car with no more serious thought than getting in on the fun, how can an instructor or a parent impress him properly with the very real dangers that confront him in driving a car?

To plant a true picture of the automobile in the public mind is a slow and arduous task. It will take at least a generation of work on the part of all of us. The most logical place to begin is with the beginning driver; and the best way to get him to view the automobile in a realistic way is to make him think. For this reason, we have stressed from beginning to end the rational, rather than the merely physical, aspects of the driving experience. So, the prime reason for stressing the intellectual components of the driving experience is to inspire the motorist to view the automobile in a fresh new light, free of the sentimental foolishness of the past.

### REMOVE FATE FROM THE DRIVER'S SEAT

But logic can serve still another function. It can attack the role that fate plays in the thinking of most motorists. The typical driver exists in a state of primitive oblivion regarding accidents. He is only too willing to place himself in the hands of fate when he drives. The reasons for this are profound and complex. But the dangers of such a psychological act are simple to perceive. It means that the driver has partially surrendered control of his own destiny on the highways.

It is this childlike invocation of fate that insists that accidents are somehow an inevitable by-product of the motoring age. And it is the primitive voice of fate that beguiles us into thinking that accidents are caused by a force beyond the hands on the steering wheel. It is this same voice of fate that sings the siren song in our ears as we hum along in the car, insisting with every throb of the wheels that accidents fall upon the unlucky and the unblessed, but will never strike us. An emphasis upon the rational element, or upon the use of common sense, in the driving experience can work to melt away this dangerous fallacy.

Common sense would insist upon the opposite and acknowledge the overwhelmingly conclusive fact that human error is the greatest source of destruction on the highways. It would, therefore, banish the notion of fate and inevitability in auto accidents. It would place responsibility for death and injury on the highway where it belongs—with us, the other fellow, with everyone who drives in the state of negligence and indifference that characterize this motoring age. So, the second aim of stressing the function of the rational is to reduce, and eventually eliminate, the role of fate in the motorist's thinking.

DRIVING WITH THE MIND

There is still a third reason for accentuating the role of the intellect in driving. This is the plain and simple fact that driving maneuvers can best be learned only within an intellectual framework. This fact is not given sufficient weight by the touring public. Most persons regard driving as a physical challenge and nothing more. It is easy to understand why: physical response are of key importance. But this is no cause to set the intellect aside, as most beginners do during the learning process.

For the truth is that there are few physical pursuits that demand so much from our understanding and judgment as driving does. Our muscular reflexes must be exercised in constant association with understanding and judgment. The automobile has become a familiar fixture of everyday life and this familiarity has bred an intellectual contempt for the complexities and hazards of its operation. This contempt can be replaced by a healthy and realistic respect only when driving is studied and learned in the appropriate rational context.

THE MIND AS THE MASTER CONTROL

And finally, it is the intellect that serves as the crux of a defensive-driving approach. Defensive driving demands that the mind be constantly in gear, so to speak. It should serve as the master control, presiding over all of our actions on the road. For it is only through the exercise of the imagination that the hazards of the road can be mentally catalogued and only through an exercise of judgment that these data can be applied to specific defensive-driving problems. So, for these various reasons, we have given the intellect a dominant role in our text.

We have gone to considerable length to make this point, because instruction in driving is basically dangerous unless it is subordinated to the control of the intellect. Every day throughout the country drivers are being licensed and sent forth on the highways without proper indoctrination concerning the hazards they will encounter. The average driver has been duped into a false sense of security by the collective notion that "There's really nothing to it." Driving a modern, high-speed automobile is almost as difficult as flying a light plane. Yet few motorists entertain the same degree of respect for the automobile as a pilot has for his plane.

Can you imagine the chaos in the airways if pilots flew as

the average motorist drives? The situation would be intolerable, and controls would be brought to bear upon it. But look at the chaos on the highways today. There is an unbelievable lack of order and discipline. Each driver seems to speed along at a deadly clip with no real, active grasp of the hazards that inhere in his every thoughtless maneuver.

### GOING BACK OVER THE ROAD

It has been the purpose of this book to suggest a solution to this dilemma through defensive driving. All along the way, we have attempted to outline a blueprint for this remedy. To begin with, we laid down a program for a defensive-driving approach. Then, we pointed out the need to purge the mind of strong emotions that prevent an evaluation of our own performance behind the wheel. Once the mind has been wiped clean of arrogance and fear, it is free to function as the control center for defensive driving. We then indicated the way that natural physical laws, our own senses, and the mechanics of the controls affect our driving. We went on to describe the basic maneuvers, all in terms that would train the mind to dominate the physical functions involved in driving.

Particular emphasis was placed upon the role of proper vision. Getting a driver to use his eyes properly is the most difficult problem facing an instructor. Some motorists can never be trained to do this. In many daily pursuits, we become conditioned to looking closely, particularly when our unconscious mind is troubled with an unformulated sense of danger, as it is in driving. Safety seems to lie in a careful scrutiny of what is right in front of us. Many drivers spend most of their energy behind the wheel staring at the hood for this reason. It gives them a sense of security, but it is a false one.

We have tried to drive home the point that a driver's safety lies in looking up and out, and in allowing his fringe or peripheral vision to spot any hazards to either side.

### INTERNAL AND EXTERNAL HAZARDS

We have insisted that a defensive driver's key responsibility is to defend life and limb from all hazards. These hazards fall into two general categories—the internal and the external. The sources of internal hazards are many. The major one is a negative frame of mind. This could include anger, tension, fear, indifference, and arrogance. One or the other of these emotions has been found to play a part in the majority of accidents. Another source of internal hazards is incomplete mastery of the controls. Still another would be the improper use of our faculties, such as our vision. And finally, internal hazards could also stem from a defect in the vehicle. A defensive driving approach calls for a rigorous and continual assessment of these hazards and the active attack of inteligence to eliminate them.

The external hazards do not fall so readily under our personal control; but they can be countered by a knowledge of what they are and an anticipation of when they might occur. The most formidable external hazard is the faulty driving of others. This may take an almost infinite variety of forms. It could be a car following too close, or one passing on a hill or changing direction into your path without a signal. It would be impossible to categorize all of the possible driving errors that threaten a motorist. The most important thing is to adopt the frame of mind that anticipates them. Here is where the intelligence plays its key role. The mind must continually come to grips with and actively imagine what might happen. It must be constantly on the alert. It must be aware of the areas of greatest danger. It must constantly school itself in

observed driving errors and mentally rehearse defensive maneuvers to counteract them.

## A LOOK TO THE FUTURE

There is little that can be done about the so-called veteran
motorist who has been led to believe that driving entails no
more than a mastery of the controls. These motorists are causing havoc on the highways today and, in the main, they will
continue to do so. The average motorist is the recipient of a
great deal of luck. He reads into his own survival an unques-
tioning faith that he is driving safely. Those who have learned
at first-hand the terrors of typical driving habits are either
dead or muted beyond hope of warning others. But the new
or beginning driver can be alerted to what will befall him
should he blindly pursue the false notions that abound in the
realm of driving. He should be warned prior to and during
the learning experience that our highways are a more dangerous jungle than ever before.

The best way to do this is through a thoroughly defined
teaching formula, one similar to that used in the field of amateur aviation. With the increase in the number of formal
driving schools throughout the country, it is hoped that such
an approach is now a possibility and will eventually become
a reality. *Your Driving Eye* is intended to alert those who
drive and those who teach driving to the problems that confront the motoring public. If a defensive-driving approach
were generally adopted tomorrow, the lives saved upon the
highways during the coming year would be more numerous
than those saved in the year following the discovery of the
Salk vaccine.

Admittedly, the American motoring public will have to
travel a long way to emerge from the present period of chaos
and carnage to the happier time that will find our highways
truly safe.

But this historic change will not be wrought by improvements in our cars or highways. It will be brought about within the collective mind of the American motorist, or it will not come about at all. The alternative to it is the present deplorable pattern of needless death and injury on the nation's highways.

It is the author's fervent hope that *Your Driving Eye* will prove to be of assistance in reducing death and damage on our highways.

## DATE DUE

| | | | |
|---|---|---|---|
| F | | | |
| MAY 12 '64 | | | |
| SEP 26 '66 | | | |
| DEC 1 '66 | | | |
| APR 26 '67 | | | |
| F | | | |
| APR 20 '81 | | | |
| | | | |
| | | | |
| | | | |
| | | | |
| | | | |
| | | | |
| | | | |
| | | | |
| | | | |
| | | | |
| | | | |
| GAYLORD | | | PRINTED IN U.S.A. |